An Architectural Handbook
of Glastonbury Abbey.

GLASTONBURY ABBEY IN 1757.

An Architectural Handbook

OF

Glastonbury Abbey

WITH A HISTORICAL CHRONICLE OF THE BUILDING

BY

Frederick Bligh Bond

F.R.I.B.A.

Hon. Diocesan Architect for Bath and Wells

Director of Excavations at Glastonbury Abbey
on behalf of the Somerset Archaeological Society

RESEARCH INTO LOST KNOWLEDGE
ORGANIZATION

c/o Mrs Janette Jackson,
36 College Court, Hammersmith,
London W6 9DZ

Distributed by
THORSONS PUBLISHERS LIMITED
Wellingborough, Northamptonshire

First published 1909
This Edition 1981

Foreword © KEITH CRITCHLOW
& JANETTE JACKSON 1981

ISBN 0 902103 06 7

Printed in Great Britain by
Nene Litho, Earls Barton, Northamptonshire
and bound by
Weatherby Woolnough, Wellingborough,
Northamptonshire

Preface to the Second Edition.

I N offering to the public this Handbook of Glastonbury Abbey the author has designed to present in a concise form a body of material of value to the architectural student, and at the same time to deal with this in a manner most likely to be serviceable and attractive to the general reader, or to the visitor who may not be versed in the technicalities of building.

Owing to the very advanced stage of dilapidation in which the fabric has come down to us, there is a difficulty, very serious in the minds of some, in apprehending the true form and extent of the original buildings, and the mutual relation of the fragments now so widely sundered. That difficulty, this handbook is designed to meet as far as may be possible. It is hoped, therefore, that the descriptions it contains may, with the aid of the specially designed illustrations, enable the reader to obtain a good grasp of the general form, and provide a framework in which his memories of the detail of the Ruins may be set.

The work embodies an outline of the results of research and excavation made during the past three years, and much new material will be found included in the new edition now offered to the public.

The diagrams of reconstruction are based upon a careful study of existing remains, and a comparison of many fragments; the light given by a study of contemporary buildings having a certain influence on this work, and that shed by documentary evidence. These, taken together, have furnished data for inductions which it is hoped may prove of value, since they have a logical sanction.

The text has undergone careful revision, and a good deal of fresh matter has been added, notably with regard to the excavations. The author's tentative reconstruction of the XVI century interior now finds a place in the volume, and the pictorial projection of the Ruins on the plan is now supplemented by an outline reconstruction of the whole exterior, which whilst largely conjectural may assist the reader in realising something of the ancient proportions of the Abbey Church, and the various periods of the fabric. Some excellent photographs are added by Mr. Everard, and a few additional sketches of detail are incorporated in the text.

The author's cordial thanks are given to the friends who have assisted him in the production of this work; to Colonel William Long, in whose library the valuable record giving the dimensions of the Edgar Chapel was discovered; to Mr. J. Allen Bartlett; Revd. G. W. Saunders; Mr. John Merrick; Mr. A. M. Broadley and to the Trustees of the Abbey for facilities for research; and to the friends who guaranteed the first cost of publication, in particular to M.. A. F. Somerville, to whose active help the original enterprise was due.

Fredk. Bligh Bond.

Bath, *Aug. 1910*

Preface to the Third Edition

BOTH the subject of this handbook and the author have been a source of inspiration for a new generation of the British heritage. What remains of the building itself stands on a deeply venerated and ancient site and it is this aspect of the Glastonbury area that attracted Bligh Bond to commence a life-long study in depth of Glastonbury Abbey.

This handbook represents the fruits of his knowledge, insight, experience and authority of the site as Diocesan Architect of Bath and Wells and Director of Excavations from 1908-1919 for the Somerset Archaeological Society.

Bond was already established as a national figure for his contribution to the Nation's heritage by the two volume study of "Rood Screens and Rood Lofts", a work shared with Dom Bede Camm, O.S.B., which was a mark of this remarkable man's consistent effort to avoid the personalised pitfalls of "self-revelation". His understanding of the Abbey historically, proportionally and geographically, as well as his substantial restoration work of the St. Mary Chapel is exceptional, so exceptional, indeed, that some of his findings were a source of both misunderstanding and eventual open hostility in certain quarters.

It was a sign of the times that so little was known about the virtual origins and sacred sciences of Gothic proportions and dimensions transmitted through the oral tradition — thus uncommitted to writing — which led Bond's adversaries to feel obliged to reject certain of his hypotheses.

One important example was the investigation, development and application of the sacred science of Gematria,[1] a subject described by one modern authority in his history of numbers and number words as the least investigated of traditional sciences.[2] This science which has difficulties for those without a transcendental dimension to their premises, yet which is a part of the revelation tradition of humanity, finds its counterpart in the Sacred Vedic, Judaic and Islamic traditions, the last having as many as nine different varieties according to S. H. Nasr[3].

Bond worked closely with the Rev. Simcox Lea, D.D., and published two remarkable little books on this subject. The work reflected his integral approach whereby he co-ordinated the 'word' the measure and the proportions of the Abbey from the precise measurements he made on the ground.

The present writers are not in a position to be able to pass judgment on some of the techniques that Bond employed, including the services of what appear to be reputed psychic sensitives, but it is equally apparent that there were bound to be those that would do so[4]. Maybe Bond should have remained diplomatically silent as to the sources of certain indications which he received, but this is hardly in the spirit of the scientist[5] of the day who is virtually obliged to publish findings, when they occur. Certainly Bond obtained significant results from the messages he received.

These more mysterious aspects of his work will provoke discussion for many a year to come, but sight must not be lost of the contribution they did so make to our understanding of Glastonbury Abbey.

His proposals for its unfoldment in time from the most ancient Mary Chapel to the Edgar Chapel climax are well argued and displayed. An inevitability marked the relationships between the parts and the whole, certain dimensions in which Bond believed, thus confirming his original intuitions and justifying the devotion which he spent on the Abbey structure.

Certainly we owe to him and to his dedicated life's work a new veneration of this sacred site; a new and deeper insight into the meaning of sacred proportion. A renewed and highly disciplined review and re-working of the Science of Gematria; finally, a new study of English history which is both unconventional and stimulating. Bond was a scrupulous worker resisting both the temptation of empty claims or the lure of wild speculation.

We have here this beautiful little Architectural Handbook into which he poured his extensive yet modestly held wisdom, as a reminder of his work. Let us hope that the Abbey will be enhanced by its re-publication and that a new look will be taken as to its implications, together with his conclusions as to the meaning of the length of the nave and the Edgar Chapel.

The Council and members of R.I.L.K.O. would like to offer this reprint as an acknowledgement of the valued inspiration which they have received from Frederick Bligh Bond.

Keith Critchlow
Janette Jackson

November 1980

(1) See R.I.L.K.O. "Gematria" and "The Apostolic Gnosis".
(2) "Number Words and Number Symbols" a cultural history of numbers, Karl Menninger, MIT Press, New York, 1970.
(3) See his "Science and Civilisation of Islam".
(4) Had he but left dated and signed affidavits of these messages as they were received, none could have suggested that they followed the finds.
(5) We use the word "science" in the traditional sense which is those human activities which deal with objective matter in a disciplined sense and whose overall objective is the integration of the human psyche.

Table of Contents.

List of Illustrations.

"Thy servants think upon her stones, and
it pitieth them to see her in the dust."

Ps. 102, v. 14, Prayer Bk. version.

There was a little city, and few men within it; and there came a great king
against it, and beseiged it, and built great bulwarks against it:
Now there was found in it a poor wise man, and he by his wisdom delivered
the city; yet no man remembered that same poor man.
Then said I, Wisdom is better than strength; never-the-less the poor man's
wisdom is despised, and his words are not heard.
The words of wise men are heard in quiet more than the cry of him that ruleth
among fools.

ECCLESIASTES. ch. 9: 14-17

An Architectural Description

of the

Abbey of Glastonbury.

CHAPTER I.

INTRODUCTORY.

LASTONBURY is the one great religious found-
dation of our British forefathers in England which
has survived without a break the period of
successive conquests of Saxon and Norseman,
and its august history carries us back to the time of the
earliest Christian settlement in Britain.

Thus it stands alone as a connecting link with the
British Church. Here alone the Celtic element has lived on
under the rule of the Saxon, and the traditions of both races
have been assimilated. Here, without breach of continuity,
the Saxon priest officiated at the same altar as the British
priest, and the Norman followed him.

The tradition which ascribes to Joseph of Arimathea
and his companions, the building of the first little church
of wattle work is a familiar one.* All through the era of

---

* John of Glaston's Hist : (Ed Hearne) I pp. 1 10, & 48 : also Malmesbury's 'Gesta
Pontificorum' Ed Hearne, pp. 5, 12. The story is that Joseph, the companion
of St. Philip, together with eleven other disciples of that apostle, introduced the
Christian religion into this country at Glastonbury circa 63 A.D., and obtained
permission to settle there from the British King Arviragus, who gave them each
a 'hide' of land; the whole forming the district known as the 'Twelve Hides
of Glaston.' [See also Polydore Vergilius Hist: fol. Basileae 1557, lib. iv. p. 89.]

Celtic dominance this humble structure was scrupulously preserved, and there appears good reason for its reputed sanctity
in the fact that it was always the object of so jealous a
regard on the part of its early occupants.

When Saxon Christianity, early in the VII century,
here replaced the old British worship, no less a measure of
care and veneration was accorded it. It is indeed a striking
testimony to the sanctity of the place that a body of religionists
having no racial sympathies or affinities with the conquered
tribes should not only have preserved, but have taken pains
to perpetuate a structure so rude and so time-worn as the
"vetusta ecclesia." Yet we read that Paulinus, Archbishop
of York, in the early part of that century, viewed the church
as a sacred object, and protected it by an external roofing of
lead, and a casing of boards.

And, following the Saxons, the Norman occupants of
Glastonbury seem to have been equally scrupulous in cherishing
the ancient fabric : and this, although as a rule they were great
innovators, and prone to despise the humbler works of the conquered English, which they usually made haste to supersede by
erecting in their stead others of far superior size and magnifi-
cence. So the old church, though doubtless renewed by
countless efforts at repair, and the slow substitution of parts,
was yet standing when the great fire of 1184 A.D. supervened,
and swept it completely away.

This fire, destructive as it was, cannot be regarded as
an unmixed evil, since it has been the means of giving us the
perfect and beautiful work whose remains still stand to attest
the skill and inspiration of its builders, and the intensity of
their veneration for the sacred spot.

Indeed, were further proof desired of the reality of those
sublime traditions which men from earliest times had associated
with this place, it should be looked for not merely in the
written records and traditions, but also and perhaps chiefly, in
the work which survives to testify to the reality of the faith
and enthusiasm of its builders.

The principal documentary record of the existence of the
wattle church in the primitive era is the chronicle of William
of Malmesbury, who was employed in the XII century to
collect evidence and write the history of Glastonbury. He tells

us of its building, and of the growth and development of the religious foundation, but his account, though doubtless based on fact, is intermixed with legend, and altered by the interpolations of later writers.

That which has been considered as the earliest piece of real history is the grant of Gwrgan, the King of Damnonia, in 601 A.D., who gave the land of Ynyswitrin, to the *old church,* in the time of the Abbot Worgret.* It is Gwrgan's gift which first makes the island a monastic island, and Professor Freeman gives sound reasons for believing that the document, which Malmesbury copied, was a genuine one. As regards the ancient name of this settlement, he thinks that the name Avalon is as old as the time when the fame of Arthur had become great, and probably older,† whilst the name Ynyswitrin is certainly older, and occurs in Malmesbury's History of the Kings, as well as in a note at the end of the life of Gildas.

Early in the eighth century we have further evidence of the existence of the wattle or wooden church in the Charter of Ine, King of the West Saxons, which is dated as having been signed in this "Lignea Basilica," or "wooden church," A.D. 725. This charter was framed to exempt the church of Glastonbury and its belongings from all outside jurisdiction, ecclesiastical or royal, and especially from the control of the local Bishops. But this very question was for over 400 years in dispute between the Monks of Glastonbury and the Bishops of the Diocese. (Collinson Hist. of Somerset, ii. p. 241.) If this Charter then existed it appears that the Bishops at least did not attach much importance to it. Moreover it presents internal marks of a spurious composition.‡

The survival of the old wooden church in the eleventh century is moreover attested by the Charter of King Cnut, A.D. 1032, also signed within its walls.‖

William of Malmesbury further tells us that a second church was built to the eastward of the first by St. David, Bishop of Menevia (d. 546) ; and a third the work of twelve

---

* The date is in the period of the mission of Saint Augustine.
† The root appears to be Semitic.
‡ J. Britton, Hist: of Wells Cathedral, 1824 edn. p 8.
‖ Cartulary of Glastonbury; Bodleian Library.

holy men, anchorites from the north of Britain, which also stood to the east of the "vetusta ecclesia." *

These churches were doubtless small in size, and probably formed a group, like those we see remaining in Celtic districts, such as Glendalough in County Wicklow.† It must be remembered that as long as Celtic religious systems, and the building traditions connected with them prevailed in these islands, our monks did not dwell or worship as a community under one roof, but followed the Eastern model of living in detached cells nearly adjoining. So that for many centuries Glaston would have been the abode of such a fellowship of holy men, forming perhaps three or four communities, each with their separate church and single habitations for each monk.

Clearer light of history begins to dawn upon Glastonbury at the commencement of the eighth century, when Ine, King of the West Saxons, gave his Charter to the Monastery, and built a new church in honour of our Lord and the Apostles Peter and Paul. Ine's church was probably on a much larger scale, but nothing remains for our enlightenment on the subject of its plan or architectural character.‡ The Saxons in their mode of church building approached more nearly the Western European model, and large churches, wherein religious communities were sheltered, were habitual with them. But monastic communities were not finally ordered and regularised in England until the ninth or tenth century, when under Dunstan, the Benedictine rule was introduced and speedily became prevalent.

---

* The number twelve recalls the practice of the older Druidical Schools, with whose tenets and practices the native Christianity of this period seems to have been blended. The Druid priests were in companies of twelve, and their priestly orders were in three degrees, as in christian Britain. J. Yarker (Arcane Schools, p. 26), says: The British or Celtic Druids were a priesthood that had features common to the Eastern Magi. Strabo said that they practised the same religious rites as did the Greek ' Cabiri,' the priest-architects who at Samothrace perpetuated the venerated traditions of the great Cyclopean builders of a time more remote. The Cabiric rites embodied the drama of a murdered God. In the Irish legend it was Saer who was killed with his twelve companions and O'Brien says that he was a 'Guabhres' or Cabiri, the name Saer signifying the Son of God. It has been held by some that the Druidical priesthood had their origin in Chaldea, whence both Phoenicians and Hebrews profess to have migrated. According to Jean Reynaud (l'Esprit de la Gaule), the mission of Druidism was (like Judaism) to uphold the idea of the Unity of God, and they did not disappear till this was accomplished.

† Ireland gives us other examples, as at Killaloe, Clonmacnois, and Cashel ; and Scotland at St. Andrew's.

‡ Save as described below (p. 14).

Dunstan is believed to have initiated some building works, but of what nature, or to what extent is not clear. We know that with the help of the Kings Edmund and Edgar* he repaired that which had been ruined or fallen to decay in the period of desolation ensuing on the Danish incursions.

The benefactions to the abbey on the part of King Edgar "the Peaceable," were great, and were never forgotten by the monks. To the very last they honoured him, and the last two Abbots built and completed a glorious chapel to receive his remains. These had been enshrined in the abbey ever since his death, A.D. 975. He was commonly regarded as a Saint, and thus spoken of, though never canonised.

Two more landmarks in the history of bygone foundations remain to be noticed ere we touch the period of surviving buildings, These are the churches erected by Turstin and Herlewin, the first and second Norman Abbots.

Turstin, who became Abbot in 1082, in succession to the Saxon Ailnoth, is said to have commenced the building of a church which was pulled down by his successor Herlewin, who thought it of insufficient size and dignity.† Herlewin was Abbot from A.D. 1101 to 1120; Malmesbury tells us that he spent £480 upon his church—a good sum for those days. It is probable that he lived to complete his work, since no addition thereto is recorded of his successor, the Abbot Henry de Blois.

In the course of the excavations made during the autumn of 1908, at the west end of the nave of the Abbey Church, a massive foundation, five feet in width, was found running parallel with the existing west wall and immediately in contact with it. This foundation turns eastward at a point a few feet north of the respond at the northern extremity of the existing fragment of the west wall, which indicates the position of the old arcade on the north side of the present nave, and it has been traced eastward for some twenty feet. It lies

---

* Wm. of Malmesbury. Gest. Pont. p. 254. Osborn. 'De vita Dunstani.' p. 100.
  In this work it is stated that Dunstan completed a great church and set of monastic offices. This would be the church which afterwards witnessed the riotous scene under Turstin for that unhappy event occurred in the first year of his abbacy. We know it was an aisled church with a triforium.

† Turstin only commenced a church. He used Dunstan's, and it was probably Dunstan's church which Herlewin pulled down.

at a depth of no less than nine feet below the grass of the nave, and measures several feet in width by two feet or more in depth.

Upon it may be seen standing a piece of masonry of very different character, and probably later in date, shewing a number of rectangular set-offs. This appears to constitute the north-west angle of one of the older churches—probably Herlewin's—whilst there is nothing inherently unreasonable in supposing that the foundation below may be a relic of Dunstan's, or even of Ine's church, though the former is by far the more probable.

The angle of masonry resting upon it contains fragments of dressed stone, worked to a convex outline, apparently parts of some massive cylindrical piers. One of them shews the head of a small niche or recess, sunk into the masonry of the pier. These would be suggestive of fragments of Dunstan's church used up by Herlewin.

Lying about amongst the loose fragments of which so great a number still exist in the abbey, may be seen here and there a piece of Norman work. One or two shew the " cushion " form of cap, characteristic of the earlier Romanesque work, and these are undoubtedly remains of the churches of the Norman Abbots. In Warner's " Glastonbury " (Plate XIII) are engravings of two exquisite pieces of Romanesque detail. One of these still survives, and is preserved in the abbey grounds. It is cut in a hard blue slate or lias stone.*

Mention may here be made of certain objects which, according to William of Malmesbury, were contained in the old church of Herlewin. First there was an ancient altar (probably the High Altar) over which were paintings of the first three Abbots, with their names, viz. : Worgret, Lademund, and Bregoret, and to this the chronicler appeals as evidence of the great antiquity of the foundation.† This

---

* Several more of these beautiful fragments have recently come to light, and are carefully preserved by the Trustees. They were found built into the foundation of a pier in the north transept, and from their propinquity to the site of the east wall of the earlier church, may be deemed to have once formed part of a rich arcading, or range of stone stalls, with twisted shafts, encircling the apse of the older building.

† W of M. De Antiq. Glast. (Lomax) p. 64.

Altar was adorned by Abbot Brihtwin, before his election to the see of Wells in 1027, with a table of gold and silver work in ivory.* Two or three crucifixes are mentioned, one of which was a gift from King Edgar.

There was also an image of the Virgin, which is said to have survived the great fire of 1184. Two or three other images are also mentioned, to which miraculous powers were attributed. The old church also undoubtedly contained the tombs of King Edgar (d. 975 A.D.) King Edmund (d. 946 A.D.). who was buried under the tower of the abbey church on the right (south) side,† and King Edmund Ironside, whose bones lay before the altar.

The latter record may be regarded as implying probably that the church was cruciform, with a central tower and north and south transepts. This was James Parker's opinion. The remains of King Edgar, first interred " in the chapter-house at the door of the church," were removed some forty years later according to Malmesbury, and placed in a casket upon the altar, together with the head of St. Apollinaris, and the relics of St. Vincent. The body of King Edmund Ironside (d. 1016 A.D.) was buried, according to the same authority, in front of the High Altar of Herlewin's church.

The records of the burial of Abbots in the older church are but scanty. That of Abbot Tica (temp: 754 A.D.), is the first spoken of, and it is described as being in the corner of the " Ecclesia major " close by the entrance into the " Ecclesia vetusta," and as being remarkable both for its size and the skill displayed in its vaulting.‡ The existence of this tomb at the time that William of Malmesbury's treatise was written, seems proof that it was preserved throughout the successive building operations of Dunstan, Turstin and Herlewin. The description also seems to imply the existence of a connecting link, an approach, or passage, between the western wall of the older abbey church and the " Vetusta Ecclesia."

As regards the tomb and relics of Dunstan, the descriptions embodied in Malmesbury's chronicle are of doubtful

* ibid p. 104.
† ibid p. 59.
‡ W. of M. De Antiq. (Lomax) p. 85. J. Parker in Som: Arch: Soc: Proc. XXVI p. 56.

authenticity. **Readers** are referred to his chronicle for this story, which is a romantic one.

There are records of four more abbots, and a monk whose tombs were in Herlewin's church, namely Brihtwin (d. 1034), who was also Bishop of Wells, and who was buried on the north side, in the apsidal chapel (Porticus) of St. John Baptist; the monk Brihtwald (d. 1045), some time Bishop of Salisbury, buried with Brihtwin; Abbots Turstin and Herlewin, both buried in the Chapel of St. Andrew, which Parker conjectures to have been an apsidal chapel on the south side of the chancel, corresponding to that of St. John Baptist on the north. This dedication would more or less correspond in position with that given to the south-east chapel of the choir of the later church of which John of Glaston speaks, and Leland describes the position, when he says that Abbot John of Breynton's tomb was in the south aisle adjoining the presbytery, before the chapel of St. Andrew.

Yet another Abbot did much building in the period before the building of the last great abbey church. This was Henry of Blois, of whom Adam de Domerham says that " he built from the foundations a Bell Tower, Chapterhouse, Cloister, Lavatory, Refectory, Dormitory, and Infirmary with its Chapel; a beautiful and ample palace; a handsome exterior gateway of squared stones; a large brewhouse; many stables for horses, and other works; besides giving various ornaments to the church."

In the times of this abbot we have again distinct evidence of the existence of the old wooden church, as it is recorded that he gave an annuity for the maintenance of a wax candle to burn perpetually before the image of the Virgin Mary, in the "vetusta ecclesia."

Malmesbury tells us that the bodies of S.S. Gildas, Patrick, Indractus, and others, were buried in the " vetusta ecclesia," and in Adam de Domerham's Chronicle, we are informed that after the fire of 1184, the bodies of the same Saints were dug up and placed in shrines. This seems an additional proof of the persistence of the ancient fabric down to the period of the fire.

The great fire, which occurred on the 25th May, 1184.*
swept away all the churches and monastic buildings save the
bell tower built by Abbot Henry; a chamber; and a chapel
built by Abbot Robert.

Thus perished the " vetusta ecclesia,' then venerable
with the weight of, perhaps one thousand years; thus perished
also the great abbey church of Herlewin, and the fine range of
buildings which Abbot Henry had caused to be built.†

---

*Roger de Hovenden: Annales. p. 624. Savile.

†The present Gateway of the Abbey is not that of Abbot Henry, but a much later
  work, whose date, though it cannot be fixed with precision, would appear by the
  character of the moulded archway to be of the earlier part of the XIV century.
  The great wall which enclosed the abbey grounds was probably co-eval. Some
  portions of this are still standing.

The Architectural Chronicle
of the Abbey from A.D. 1184.

CHAPTER II.

HE Abbey at the time of the fire was in the custody of King Henry II. who kept the revenues in his own hands, and it was under his auspices that there arose the great scheme of building whose remains we now see. The work was commenced forthwith, the direction being committed to Radulphus Fitz Stephen, the King's Chamberlain.

The Church (or Chapel) of St. Mary was the first to be built, on the site of the old wooden church, and approximately to its original dimensions. Adam de Domerham tells us that this building was dedicated by Reginald, Bishop of Bath, on St. Barnabas' Day *about* the year 1186. The uncertainty about the year allows us to assume that 1187 A.D., may have been the actual date, since the fire occurred only three years before, and a considerable time would be required to mature so elaborate and beautiful a scheme. The building, however, was probably not entirely completed until much later.

The Chapel of St. Mary (see general plan) is the building first seen on approaching the ruins. It stands at the western end of the enclosure, and forms the extreme limit of a very elongated group. The Chapel was originally a detached rectangular building, independent of the main structure. but is now linked to the ruins of the great Abbey Church by a continuation known as the 'Galilee' which will be hereafter described. The distinction between the Chapel of St. Mary and the Galilee will be easily discerned, not only by the comparatively perfect state of the former, but by the great difference in their design and style of architecture.

The building of the " Ecclesia major " or great Abbey Church was commenced about the same time as that of the Chapel, as appears by a Charter of King Henry II, which, if authentic, must have been signed between December 2nd, and December 17th, 1184, since the names of Baldwin, Archbishop of Canterbury, and Bartholomew, Bishop of Exeter, are among the signatories. The earlier date is that of Baldwin's election ; the later that of Bartholomew's decease.

For five years the work, under the control of Radulphus, and with royal support, made great progress, the intention clearly being to create a building of one style from end to end, like Salisbury ; and it appears that the architect must have built to an entirely new plan, on a greatly increased scale, sweeping away all the old work, and retaining nothing for re-use saving, possibly, a certain number of worked stones exhibiting the finely carved chevron enrichment characteristic of the Anglo-Norman work of the earlier XII century.

The words of Adam de Domerham's record, written A.D. 1280-90, may here be quoted : " He (Fitz Stephen) " repaired all the offices, and afterwards laying the foundations " of a most beautiful church, carried them to the length of four " hundred feet, and to the width of eighty feet. Pressing on " rapidly with the work he spared no expense. What he could " not obtain from Glastonbury, that the Royal Bounty supplied. " Into the foundations of the church were put also the stones " of that great palace which Abbot Henry built, as well as those " of the wall of the courtyard. Thus having built a good part " of the church he would have completed the rest, if God had " prolonged the King's life. But, alas ! death, covetous, and " too watchful, snatched him away, and thus inflicted another " wound upon the monks, who were only just recovering from " their last misfortune."

In 1189 A.D., King Henry died and the work was stopped. Ralph Fitz Stephen, in whose charge the works were, is believed to have died also about this time, and the undertaking thus received a total check, nothing further being attempted by the next Abbot (Henry de Soully, appointed c. 1191). It is not known how far the work of building the original walls of the church may have progressed during the first active building period under Henry II. but the aisle walls were most probably completed, together with the arcades, to the height of the first stage. On the promotion of this Abbot to the see of Worcester, the monks elected William Pyke, who was promptly excommunicated by Bishop Savaric and his abbey placed under an interdict. Then followed the troublous times of King John's reign, during which the Abbey was involved in disputes, and was mulcted of much of its property. But when Henry III came to the throne, a further era of activity and prosperity dawned.

When Savaric became Bishop of Wells (1192-1206) he annexed the Abbey to the Bishopric, assuming the title of Bishop of Glastonbury, and the Papal confirmation of this act gives him "all those houses near the Chapel of St. Mary which belonged to the Abbot, together with the enclosure by the wall which extends from the larder, to the corner of the said chapel, and he shall be allowed to make his portal towards the Market Place of Glastonbury." This is the situation of the old gateway recently restored, and now used as an entrance to the Abbey.

In 1218 A.D., the monks received permission to elect their own Abbot, and chose William Vigor, who for five years was their master. He was no builder, and his benefactions to the Abbey took the form of improvements in the personal comfort of the monks.

This Abbot was buried in the older Chapter-house. The Revd. C. L. Marson is inclined to the opinion that the effigy which now stands against the wall in the Abbots' Kitchen is of this Abbot.* But it is on record that the figure in the Kitchen was dug up in the north aisle of the Abbey in the year 1780.†

During the time of Robert de Bath (Abbot 1223-1234) the Abbey was poor, and no building was done, but in 1235 Michael of Ambresbury, a man of good business ability, was elected, and during his eighteen years of rule, brought the establishment out of poverty into prosperity, He erected a hundred buildings, some within, some without, the monastery, and probably did something to the church, but what, is not recorded, He was buried in the north transept of the great

---

* Glastonbury : The English Jerusalem (1909) p. 103.
† Carter's "Specimens of Gothic Architecture" 1824, p. 53.

church, which must therefore have been completed before A.D. 1255.

Abbot Roger Ford who succeeded him, appears to have done no building. He was Abbot for five years, and was buried at Westminster. Abbot Robert Petherton, who followed in 1260, is also among those of whom no building works are recorded. He died in 1274, and was buried in the north transept before the altar of St. Thomas the Martyr, on the left hand of Abbot Michael.* From this we gather that one of the two altars in the north transept chapels was dedicated to the Martyr of Canterbury—and this was probably in the beautiful chapel still standing.

John de Tantonia (Taunton) was next Abbot, and the chief event of his tenure of office was the visit of Edward I and his Queen in 1278, when, after many imposing functions the Abbot entertained the Royal party, and proceeded to the tomb of King Arthur, whose bones, with those of his Queen, were duly discovered and placed in a shrine before the High Altar in the Choir. This was done on the 19th of April, 1278. The placing of these relics was in all probability a work connected with the consecration of the High Altar, and assists us to fix the date of the completion of the original choir. Adam de Domerham's story ends with the death of Abbot John of Taunton in 1291. From Leland we find that this Abbot was buried next the other two, in the North Transept.

During the Abbacy of John of Taunton, the work of completion must have proceeded rapidly. The unity of style, had so far been preserved in a manner remarkable in view of the prolonged period over which the erection of the Abbey had been spread ; and of the stoppage of the work, which lasted perhaps 50 years.† It is difficult now to discern any distinct trace of difference until we come to the west end of the Nave, where in the surviving fragment, we have a new departure in style—the Early English being substituted for the original Transitional type.

---

* Visitors to the Abbey will observe among the fragments at this spot a portion of the effigy of an ecclesiastic with part of the enriched slab supporting it.

† From 1189 to 1239 or thereabouts—This would bring us to the 4th year of the Abbacy of Michael of Ambresbury. There was a subsequent interval of 20 years during which no building is recorded.

The Galilee or western chapel was almost certainly a part of the original scheme, as this is a recognised feature of XII century buildings, but it was evidently decided, shortly after the completion of the works in the early part of the XIV century that the Chapel of St. Mary, representing the "Vetusta Ecclesia," should be thrown open to the great church, and this was done by coupling it to the Galilee, the eastern wall of St. Mary's Chapel being thrown down, and an arch substituted—the same that is now to be seen in a restored form, spanning the interior at this point.

A BRIEF SURVEY OF THE RUINS.

A glance at the plan may now be helpful in forming an accurate impression of the real relation in which the various buildings stood to one another.

Going eastwards from the Chapel of St. Mary, the Galilee is seen, and, abutting upon it, the west wall of the nave. Thence we come into the open space where once stood the majestic nave itself. Now nothing is visible except a fragment of the wall of the south aisle, containing three windows and the broken doorway to the cloister.

The rest is an uniform greensward, marked only by a grass bank, which indicates roughly the line of the transepts.* As the plan shews, the transepts formed the symmetric arms of a cross, and were each of a length sufficient to allow of two bays, or severies, projecting beyond the general line of the aisle walls on north and south. All the walls are gone except the two large fragments of the eastern face. These give us a clue to the design, as they retain portions of the clerestory and triforium arcades united with the moulded shafting of the two large piers between which stood the great choir arch. The springing of this arch can still be seen, and the curve followed by the eye for a short distance. These piers with their arch were the eastern supports of the central tower, which stood upon four such piers, forming a square of about 40 feet on plan,

* The level of the transept floor is shewn in a small fragment of encaustic tile work still remaining   This is to be seen in its original position in the north transept, and shews the double-headed eagle displayed, with one or two tiles of a foliated design adjoining.

The position of the pier at the south west angle of the square is visible in the grass bank, where the foundation is exposed.

Each transept was furnished with aisles along its east side, and these give access to two chapels running eastward, and parallel to the choir. The plan shews their position, and fortunately one of these in the north transept still survives, and may be seen immediately to the north of the archway which leads into the north aisle of the choir.

The two large piers of the choir arch still standing shew the lesser arches which led from the transepts to the aisles on the north and the south sides of the choir. They admit now to another open grassy area; and on entering the choir it will be seen that, as in the nave, the whole of the masonry of the principal walls with their pillars and arches is gone, and even the foundations of the double row of columns are not now visible. Nothing is left but the greater part of the south aisle wall, a fragment of the north side, and two smaller fragments of the east wall.

The clear internal measurement from end to end of nave and choir is about 377 feet, being 224 feet for nave and transept and 153 from the face of the transept wall eastwards. But as will presently be seen, this does not represent the earlier measurement, since the choir was elongated at a later period, and its original length was less by forty feet.

THE CHRONICLE RESUMED.

The chronicles of the building of Glastonbury Abbey bring us now to A.D. 1303, when we learn from John of Garston that Abbot Geoffrey Fromond caused the church to be dedicated. This was effected during his Abbacy (1303—1322), and the event forms a landmark in the history of the Abbey.

The transepts had long been completed; the choir also for some years. Both were used for sepulture, and the chief altars had been dedicated.

Abbot John of Kent, the predecessor of Abbot Geoffrey, was buried on the north side of the presbytery, between the pillars of the north aisle. This Abbot is recorded to have furnished the altars, and provided the necessary ornaments and vestments.

The nave of the church, at the time of the dedication, must have been in an incomplete state, furnished perhaps with a temporary roof over the four western bays, as not more than five were then vaulted. The western end had only been completed in its lower part, towards the close of the XIII. Century, and it is likely that the superstructure and western towers would be some years later in building, so that the nave would hardly have been ready for use until the early years of the XIV. Century.

Abbot Geoffrey spent a thousand pounds or more on other buildings within and without the Monastery, and began the building of the Great Hall, and under his rule the church approached completion. He was buried in the south transept.

Walter de Taunton, who succeeded him, only survived his election a few weeks, but the erection of the great choir screen is credited to him. Of this, John of Glaston says "He constructed the Pulpitum of the Church with ten images,* and erected a large cross with the Figure of our Lord and of Mary and John."

This screen crossed the choir archway between the piers still standing, and the grooves cut in the stonework by the masons to allow the fluid cement to run in and unite the faces of the masonry are still visible.

Abbot Walter de Taunton was buried, according to Leland, in the north transept, "before the image of our Lord crucified," which would imply a position near the choir arch, probably under the arch of the north transept.

The completion of the nave was effected by the next Abbot, Adam de Sodbury, who was elected on February 5th, 1323. He did much for the Abbey. We are told that he vaulted the greater part of the nave, and ornamented it with beautiful paintings, by which it appears that Abbot Fromond

---

* The discovery of a fragment of a finger carved in stone, and tinted flesh-colour, just by the foundation of this screen, suggests that these figures were probably life-size, and painted in natural colour.

24

had already completed a part, namely the eastern section. Under his rule were also provided the large clock [horologium] for which the Abbey was famous, the bells, seven in number, which were in the central tower, and five in another tower, described as the steeple [clocherio.] The central tower of the church had almost certainly been completed in the time of Abbot Fromond (1303—1322), as, if Abbot de Sodbury had been the builder, it is hardly likely that John of Glaston, who gives so ample a list of his works, would have failed to record it. Abbot de Sodbury also gave a great organ, and various altars and ornaments.*

With the death of this Abbot, which took place in 1334, we begin to hear of burials in the nave. His tomb was there, with the tombs of his father and mother, on his right and left. John of Breynton succeeded him in 1334, and he completed the Great Hall, spending £1,000. His gifts to the church were of a minor nature, for the adornment of altars.

Walter de Monyngton, who succeeded him in 1342, was another great builder, and we are told by John of Glaston that he added greatly to the monastic buildings, whilst Leland tells us that he increased the length of the Presbytery, *i.e.,* the choir, by two arches—thus making it six arches in length, in place of four. He also re-faced the interior of the choir walls and re-vaulted the whole area. The retro-choir, or space to the eastward of the high altar, containing the ambulatory or processional way, and a row of chapels behind it (see plan), was also carried out eastward by him, and the fragments of walling still visible at the east end of the choir enclosure are of his work.

Abbot Monington also built the western half of the Chapter house, which was in the position usual in Benedictine monasteries, and abutted upon the east walk of the cloisters, which were here upon the south side of the church. His work in the church itself will be dealt with in detail in the architectural chapter on the choir.

Abbot John Chinnock, who succeeded in 1374, finished Monington's work, built the Dormitory and Fratry, re-built the Cloisters, and is said by Leland to have completed the

---

* John of G., p. 263.

Chapter house, within which building he was buried, an alabaster effigy being laid over the spot. John of Glaston, however, places the credit of its completion to Abbot Nicholas Frome (1420-1456). The balance of accuracy seems in favour of Leland, but the discrepancy may be more apparant than real, as the first Abbot may have given the money, and the second carried out the work.

It was during the Abbacy of Chinnock or Frome that the Abbot's Kitchen was erected. Some authorities have designated this building as a work of the latter part of the XIV century ; others are inclined to assign a later date.

The chronicle of John of Glaston closes with the record of Abbot John Selwood (1456-1493) whose work has left no mark upon the architectural history of the Abbey Church, though evidences of his building activity are to be seen in other buildings in the neighbourhood. We are therefore dependent, in a great measure, upon Leland for our knowledge of the works of the last great builder, Abbot Richard Bere. This Abbot succeeded in 1493, and held office until 1524. The record of his works may be quoted *verbatim* from Leland,* and is as under :—

"Abbat Beere builded Edgares Chapel at the east end of the Church. But Abbat Whiting performed sum part of it."

"Bere archid on both sides the Est parte of the churche that began to cast owt."

"Bere made the volte of the steple in the transepto and under, two arches like S. Andres Crosse, *els it had fallen.*"

"Bere cumming from his Embassadrie out of Italie made a Chapelle of our Lady de Loretta, joining to the north side of the body of the Church."

"He made the chapelle of the Sepulcher in the Southe End Navis Ecclesiae, whereby he is buried sub plano marmore yn the South Isle of the Bodies of the Church."

* Leland, Itinerary, Vol. III., p. 103.

Bere died in January, 1524, and was succeeded by Abbot Richard Whiting, whose unhappy history is well known. This Abbot completed the Edgar Chapel, in the east end, but no other building work of his period is specified, though Collinson* says that he greatly improved the whole monastery.

Another work of the later period is the crypt beneath St. Mary's Chapel. This would appear to have been the work of Abbot Bere, as its architectural features are those of the early XVI century ; it appears also from Leland's record that this Abbot spent a considerable sum in miscellaneous building works, and added certain chapels and vaults to different parts of the church.

With the work of Bere and Whiting the chronicle of the building of the Abbey comes to an end.

The foundations of the chapel built by Bere to the memory of King Edgar have been disinterred since the year 1908, together with the later work, believed to have been added by Whiting, which takes the form of a polygonal apse. For a full description of these, as well as the foregoing works mentioned, the reader is referred to the architectural descriptions following, but a glance at the general plan will shew the form of the chapel and its position relatively to the main structure.

THE DESTRUCTION OF THE ABBEY.

Abbot Richard Whiting, despite the fact that he had proclaimed himself a patriotic English Churchman by signing the deed which proclaimed Henry "Supreme Head of the Church," yet fell a victim to the Royal displeasure, in that he refused to surrender his monastery, and yield up its accumulated treasure. He was therefore imprisoned, tried and barbarously executed on November 15th, 1539, together with his treasurer, Roger Jacob, and his sub-treasurer, John Thorn, both monks of the Abbey. His head was placed over the Abbey Gate, and his quartered body distributed to Wells, Bath, Ilchester and Bridgwater.

The story of Richard Whiting, last Abbot of Glastonbury, reveals him as a great symbolic figure in English Church

* Beauties of British Antiquity (1779), p. 220.

history. He confronts us as a true witness of the Catholic faith, obedient to his religion in matters spiritual, and to his King in affairs of government. Willing on the one hand to submit to the rule of his sovereign as temporal head of the English Church, he yet was courageous to resist tyranny and injustice and yielded himself to a barbarous death for love of his House and in defence of her liberties. His high character is fully recognised by Rome, whose Pontiff has beatified his memory notwithstanding the incontrovertible fact that the Abbot with all his monks had for some years before the dissolution ceased to recognise the Papal authority—that they, in fact, were Protestants, in the primary and true sense of that much perverted word. (*See Appendix*). How much rather then should one who stood for ecclesiastical liberty here, and by a definite act abjured all foreign jurisdiction, merit the honorable regard of every English Churchman of whatsoever shade of opinion he may be.

The Abbey was forfeit to the King, who sold the lands and divided the property. The buildings were given over to pillage and destruction, and the grand library scattered. In the following reign, the property having passed into the hands of the Protector Somerset, the roofs were stripped of their lead, which was carried off to Jersey, and there utilised to cover the Castle of Mount Orgueil.

In the reign of Mary, some attempt at reparation was made at the instance of local gentlemen, and had the Queen survived longer, it is probable that the ancient services would have been resumed. But Elizabeth became Queen, and the doom of the great fabric was finally sealed.

Since 1551, a colony of Flemish weavers, who had been encouraged by the Protector to settle in Glastonbury, had begun to take up their abode in the deserted buildings, and a substantial sum of money (£484 14s. or about £11 per household) was lent them in order to assist them to establish their industry. The keeper of the house in the Overwall Park (now " Worrall " or Weary-all)* was appointed their supervisor, and the park was cut up into four-acre allotments for them.

---

* Readers may prefer the alternative derivation of ' Weary-all," from the Anglo-Saxon 'Wirral ' = a pasture.

The Protector was attainted, and the Flemings fell into poverty, as a consequence of which the King appointed a Commission of five, including Bishop Barlow, to effect a settlement,

Habitations were necessary for the families lately arrived, who had swelled the total to forty-four—probably two hundred souls. We learn that but six houses were ready; twenty-two others capable of repair, but at that time lacking doors and windows. Sixteen more were needed, and towards the provision of these, the Commissioners found 'certain void rooms where houses had been'; and some walls yet standing where 'divers could be made,' within the late Monastery.*

Building operations were commenced, and a surveyor appointed. The park of "O'rwall" (as a contemporary document spells it) was converted into common grazing land, for its 200 acres were found insufficient for sub-division. In addition, the garden of two acres on the north or "house" side of the late Abbey, was allotted to those who had no other garden, and the house called the "Priory," behind the Church was appointed for the use of the Superintendent. On the south side of the Monastery were built two dye-houses, a brew-house, and a bake-house, and these were enclosed with a stone wall, The Flemings were most considerately treated, and obtained many privileges by special grant. They held their own religious services, using their own order and discipline, according to a book called "Liturgia," and were finally naturalised and by incorporation became an English Guild.† Thus they remained until Queen Mary's accession drove them away, and they went to Frankfort.

The sad history of the destruction of the great church goes on through the closing years of the XVI century, when the Nave fell into complete dilapidation. The times of the early Stuarts seem to have witnessed an ever hastening destruction, and we read of the use of gunpowder for the more speedy demolition of the fabric. But the size of the Church was so gigantic that in spite of these ruthless and viol it onslaughts a very considerable portion was surviving as l ce as Hollar's day—even, indeed, until the second decade of the XVIII century.

* State Papers, Edw. VI. vol. xiii. No. 74, and xiv, Nos. 2 and 13.
Emanuel Green, in Som. Arch. Soc. Proc. XXVI ii 22.

From the isolated situation of Glastonbury, there was a scarcity of good building stone, and the Abbey became literally a common quarry for the neighbourhood. Stones were taken for the erection of walls, sheds, farm buildings, etc., and thus scattered over a radius of many miles from the town. This lamentable state of things seems to have gone on at intervals for well over two hundred years. Not only was the excellent squared freestone a most tempting spoil for the house builder, but the rubble core of the walls, and the heavy stonework of the foundations also found their uses. It is probable that the latter material was largely utilised to form a solid foundation across the marsh land for the new causeway to Wells. But it may be that if the grounds below this roadway were examined, some treasures of architectural merit might come to light in the shape of carved and moulded freestone, deemed unsuitable in size or shape for building purposes and therefore cast into the morass.

There is at present, so far as we are aware, an entire lack of data as to the appearance of the Abbey Church in its original state,* and no plans are known to be extant. Neither have we any knowledge of the aspect of the building in the earlier stages of its dilapidation ; and it is not until the second half of the XVII century that any particulars of this nature are provided for us. Hollar's engraving, published in 1655, gives a general view of the ruins as they stood in those days, but without some corroborative data it would be difficult to determine the meaning of many of the features there shewn. All that we can say with certainty is that at that time the south aisle of the nave was to a great extent preserved, shew-ing an unbroken connection with the western end of the church ; two complete bays or nearly that amount, of the tall wall of the south transept, where now only a half bay is visible ; and probably the north side of the choir (although this is not shewn in Hollar's view, but in a later engraving published by Stukeley). Collinson, in his " Beauties of British Antiquity " published in 1779, mentions that two pillars of the Choir with a portion of the wall were then standing. Even as late as 1720 two bays of the south transept wall were left, the inner one shewing the perfect form

* The elevation on Plate XIIa claims only to be an index of the general proportions of the Abbey, and to be explanatory of the works of the several Abbots who built at various dates.

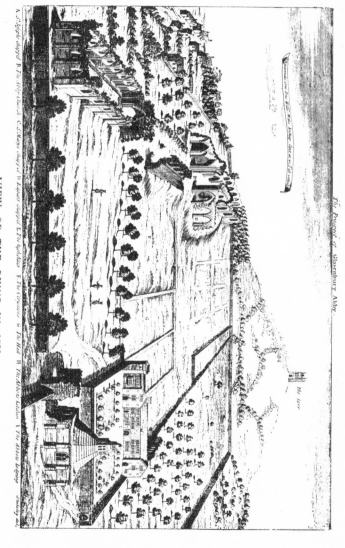

PLATE I.

VIEW OF THE RUINS IN 1723

(From Stukeley's Itinerary.)

PLATE 2.

GLASTONBURY ABBEY IN 1817 (CONEY).

of the triforium arcade, and clerestory, and the outer [restored in Plate 9] retaining still the greater portion of its members. We see it thus represented in a plate preserved in Steven's "Monasticon." In Hollar's work also the great gable wall of the Refectory, to the west, is seen, and he says that this was 80 feet high, and 58 feet wide. The correctness of the latter dimension has been proved by measurement of the excavated footings of the Refectory cellar.

Hollar states in a note on his drawing that the former buildings were so vast that what was standing in his day was but a tenth part of that which formerly existed.

About the time of Queen Anne, it is probable that all the remaining fragments of the Refectory were demolished. It is certain that some time prior to 1710 the masonry of the crypt or vault beneath it was disposed of to the inhabitants of Glastonbury for the purpose of building a Market Hall.*

Stukeley's Itinerary, published in 1723, indicates the continued presence above ground of the bases of many of the Nave piers, and he also gives us the position of the principal monastic buildings from walls remaining at that time, but so inaccurate and careless are his drawings that they are practically valueless as exact indications.

The want of good drawings of the Abbey was lamented by Hearne the antiquary, who in his Diary, under date 1718, Mar. 6, speaks of the need of a "more perfect draft published of the Ruins of Glastonbury Abbey than that in the Monasticon," a strong reason for his wish being supplied in the fact that a further era of destruction was that year being inaugurated. This author is very dissatisfied with the work of Dr. Stukeley, whom he condemns as inaccurate.

In June Hearne writes, "Mr. Gwyn says that the Puritanical possessor of Glastonbury is very busy in destroying the goodlisome Ruins of that place."

---

* An interesting record of this transaction has recently come to light in a MS. Diary, written by one John Cannon, dating from 1741 or 1742, now in the possession of Mr. Felton, of Weymouth, The Market Hall is depicted and is a plain building on arches. It seems to have been a gift to the town by William Strode, Esq, After its erection the market, hitherto prosperous, dwindled away, and the inhabitants thought it was owing to the ill fortune that attended the use of the Abbey stone.

This fact is also alluded to by Stukeley, who observes that the Abbey was, at the time of his visit, tenanted by a Presbyterian, who committed more barbarous havoc than had been made since the Dissolution, for every week a pillar, a buttress, a window joint, or an angle of fine hewn stone was sold to the best bidder. Whilst he was there, they were "excoriating St. Joseph's Chapel" for that purpose ; and the squared stones were laid up by lot in the Abbots' kitchen—the rest went to paving yards or stalls for cattle, or to the highway.*

In 1720 the Abbot's House, a building whose picturesque outlines are preserved to us in Stukeley's old engraving, was demolished by the vandal owner, and a new house built of its material. This house is the one now known as the "Abbey Grange," in Magdalen Street. It contains numerous old panels and carvings from the Abbot's House.

The work of ruin went on for some years, and in views published not long after the issue of the "Monasticon" we begin to see the walls of the Abbey assume an appearance not far different from that which they wear to-day.

We have the good fortune to be able to reproduce in colours a reduced *facsimile* of a very fine water colour sketch taken in 1757, hitherto unpublished, and now in the collection of the author, to whom it was presented by Mr. A. M. Broadley. The picture forms the Frontispiece to the title page. In view of the lapse of time—upwards of 150 years—it certainly seems amazing that the ruins have stood so well to the present day. One feature which appears in this picture is now missing—that is, the walling in the foreground on the left. These probably represent all that was then remaining of the Chapter House walls.

Some fragments of building on the north side of the Nave were surviving as recently as 1817, when Coney's

---

* The Cannon MS. alludes to this vandal tenant as "one Thomas Prew, a rank presbiterian, who pull'd down and sold vast quantities of ye stones, and rooted up ye vaults by blowing them up with gunpowder. He also pull'd down ye ancient Hall, and with the stones built a dwelling-house near ye gate called Magdalen's Gate, and placed in ye front and walls, ye arms, cyphers, and other decorations figures of ye Abbots, Priors, etc. . . and escutcheons which was once in ye old buildings, and many other stones he sold to amend ye roads and highways and to ye Townspeople with wch many houses have been built, and it was observable yt such houses so built, did not long stand, nor the possessors thrive."

drawings were published. In one of these we see a wall with a row of windows having a rather unusual detail in the heads.* (Plate 2.) This would be near the site of the " Loretto " Chapel, built by Abbot Bere. Carter, writing some few years later, tells us† that the Loretto Chapel was then standing, and if he be correct, it must have been a substantial piece of masonry exterior to the Church, and not a light internal structure within it, as has been conjectured. But he may have been referring to the chapel of Saint Thomas the Martyr in the north transept, which has sometimes been miscalled the ' Loretto Chapel.'‡

Warner, in his work on the Abbey of Glastonbury, published at about the same time, gives us a plan, based to a great extent on Stukeley's work, and indicating in dotted lines a retro-chapel eastward of the choir.

Visible evidence of this feature has doubtless been lacking for a very long time past, though it has recently come to light; but it would appear that some part of the foundations of the Edgar Chapel, including its apse, must have been in evidence as a feature of the Abbey plan, during the XVIII century. Until quite recently also there was lacking in the documentary evidence, any direct reference to this work as the ' Edgar ' Chapel, with a true series of dimensions. This has at last come to light in an old private collection.

A final period of destruction was inaugurated by one John Down, also a Presbyterian, who held the Abbey for sixty years, during the latter part of the XVIII, and the first few decades of the XIX century, and it was probably during his tenancy that the last trace of these foundations disappeared. Much was uncovered about the years 1812-13, and some scanty record has been preserved, but whatever was

---

* A sketch plan in the Cannon MS. shews a group of ruins in an apparently similar position, and he records the tradition of a very magnificent building at this point, which he terms the "Chapter House." However erroneous this designation, we may at least accept his record as corroborative of the existence of a richly-ornamented building of some special nature (as distinct from the body of the church) at the junction of the Nave aisle and North Transept.

† "Specimens," &c., p. 34, 1824 edn.

‡ Eyston writing in 1714 mentions five chapels: (1) St. Edgar's; (2) St. Mary's, in the north aisle of the Choir; (3) St. Andrew's, in the south aisle; (4) The Chapel of Our Lady of Loretto, on the north side of the nave; and (5) that of the Holy Sepulchre at the south end. "These" he says "are all the Chapels I could recover.'

then unearthed was promptly eradicated, and this fate overtook the missing piers and screen walls of the central chapels in the retro-choir—also the tiled floor in the apse of the Edgar Chapel, and fragments of its stained glass and architectural features, all of which came to light in that year.

After the death of John Down, the Abbey passed into the hands of reverent custodians, and its subsequent history has been a more fortunate one. Mr. Reeves, a late owner, did much to preserve what was left, and it was he who threw across the area of the crypt of St. Mary's Chapel the arches of plain stone which have so materially helped to prevent the subsidence to which this work was liable after the fall of the vault. That event happened, or was in process of happening, in Stukeley's time. In 1784 practically the whole of this floor had disappeared into the crypt below, and the vault was full of water, so that in the etching published by Carter at that date it has the appearance of a large pond.

This chronicle of the several vicissitudes through which the building has passed, and the progress of its dilapidation, may be fitly concluded by a reference of a congratulatory nature to those works of repair and support which by the efforts of the executive Trustees, acting for the representative Council of English Churchmen in whom the custody of the Abbey is vested, are beginning to redeem from impending ruin some of the most interesting and artistically priceless features of a building whose history and whose architecture are alike world-famous and the pride of all true Englishmen.

The Design
of the Abbey.

CHAPTER III.

VERY great building, however original in design, derives its form and detail from certain antecedent schools of architecture, from which the best elements are selected, and harmoniously blended. When this is done with consummate skill and judgment, the work marks a new stage in the history of architecture. Glastonbury Abbey is one of those buildings which mark the union of several well-defined schools of design, and these are here so skilfully interwoven as to present an architectural unity, a work of unique and undying interest, and a model for builders in stone, for all time.

In order to trace the influences which affected the creation of the Glastonbury design it will be necessary to refer to the work of contemporary builders, who from the nearness of their field of work, or from the strength of their architectural school may be deemed to have left their mark upon Glastonbury. They are as follows:—

(1). Reginald Fitz Joceline, Bishop of Wells, 1174-1191, under whom the western part of the Choir, and the eastern (and greater) part of the nave of Wells Cathedral were carried out. Before becoming Bishop, Reginald had been for some years in France, where he had imbibed some of the advanced ideas of the French schools of building.

The influence of his building methods appears most prominently in the form of the clustered piers which, in spite of differences of detail, shew in their scanty remains a distinct relationship of design. The broad lancet windows of Glastonbury are also strikingly similar to those of Wells, viewed apart from their subsequent addition of tracery.

(2). Hugh, Prior of Witham (near Wells), 1175-
1186. This great builder, better known as St. Hugh of
Lincoln, to which see he was translated in 1186-7, was a
Frenchman of noble birth, a native of Avalon in Burgundy,
who became a Carthusian monk, and so increased the fame of
his order that at the request of King Henry II., possibly
prompted by Reginald,* he came over to organise a Carthusian
House in England, and thus in 1175 became Prior of Witham,
a locality not far removed from Glastonbury, and in close
proximity to the Abbey quarries at Doulting. Here we have
a presumptive link, likely to have been a strong one during the
two years (1184-1186) which intervened between the great
fire of Glastonbury and the translation of Hugh. In this
connection it would appear likely enough that Hugh's memories
of his own Avalon might move him to some more than
ordinary degree of interest in the Avalon near at hand in the
country of his adoption, and that, granted the opportunity, such
interest might be turned to practical account.

The probable influence of Hugh is discernible most
clearly in the Chapel of St. Mary, which is in some respects of
a Burgundian type of Romanesque. It seems also apparent in
the plan of the great church, as will be shewn later, under the
heading of " The Galilee."

(3). The personal equation of Radulphus Fitz-Stephen
must be taken into account, but we do not know that he was
himself a builder, so much as a steward or comptroller of
works. His previous appointment as King's " camerarius," or
chamberlain would suggest the latter. It is recorded that King
Henry, who appointed him, gave much money to the rebuilding
of Glastonbury. Yet the King had at one time shewn himself
parsimonious where monasteries were concerned. The man
who, of all others, had most influence with him in this
direction seems to have been Hugh of Avalon, Prior of Witham,
and, if it were the King who furnished the funds for the
building, Hugh's advocacy seems probable, and his personal
activity a factor to be taken into account.

---

*Canon Church gives the whole history of the transfer of Hugh to Witham, and shews
how Bishop Reginald's consecration was hastened in order that he might under-
take the mission of inviting Hugh in the King's name (Four Somerset Bishops.
Rev. C. M. Church, M.A., F.S.A. T. Burleigh, London, 1909: p.p. 26-27).

(4). Peter de Leia: the builder of St. David s Cathedral. Until the end of the XI century this See claimed a metropolitan authority, and as the last outpost of the Celtic Church, enjoyed a precarious independence. But about 1115 A.D. it passed under the complete jurisdiction of Canterbury, and a Norman, Bernard, was consecrated Bishop. Henceforth there was closer touch between St. David's and the English Church. The Bristol Channel became more and more a highway of communication between the solitary Cathedral on its isolated and rock-bound promontory, and the busy life of the West of England. Thus the ancient and traditional link which bound Glastonbury to the founder of the See and Monastery of Menevia in the VII century was re-inforced in the XII.

The Cathedral of St. David's, which is of extraordinary interest, presents many striking architectural parallels, well worthy of attentive study; but none more remarkable than that of the earlier features and details, which abundantly recall Glastonbury.

In particular we may mention the chevron or zigzag enrichment, in diversified forms, which are of a similar nature in both works. The Nave of St. David's Cathedral was commenced A.D. 1180 by Bishop Peter de Leia; hence it was standing as a recent model, and a probable source of influence for the building of Glastonbury. The nave arches at St. David's are semi-circular, those in the choir being pointed, just as we observe in the windows at Glastonbury.

Such are the influences which were in the ascendant at the birth of the noble buildings which arose after the great fire of 1184 A.D,; those which ruled its later history were as follows:

(1). The work and personality of Jocelyn Fitz Trotman, Bishop of Wells, 1206-1242: and architect of the noble west front of his cathedral.

His work is reflected in the west end of the Nave of Glastonbury, which shews a similar arrangement, and some attempt at a reproduction of the detail. (See detailed descriptions.)

(2). The work of Ralph de Salopia, Bishop of Wells, 1329-1363, who prolonged the Choir of his Cathedral three bays, making a total of six, and refaced it internally, blocking up the "triforium" with panellings to match the new bays added, whilst at the same time the vaulted roof of unique form, with its liernes and bosses, in part intersecting angular surfaces, and in part, lying upon the uniform sweep of the "barrel" vault, was achieved, and stood as a pattern to Glastonbury builders.

This work, as will be evident in the detailed descriptions of the Glastonbury Choir, given on a later page, must have exercised a certain influence upon the work of that great contemporary builder Walter Monington, Abbot of Glastonbury, 1342-1374, but mingled with this appears that of another and even more powerful exemplar—the architectural genius who created the choir of Gloucester Cathedral.

(3). The infuence of Gloucester. Between the years 1337-1340 the transformation of the Choir from a plain Norman structure of round arches and simple mouldings to the elaborate and beautiful "Perpendicular" work we see now, was effected; and was destined to revolutionise the architecture of England.*

The new style was everywhere adopted, and in place of the flowing tracery of the Edwardian period was substituted the stiff vertical lines of the "Perpendicular," whilst plain surfaces were adorned with a network of small upright panels and all the customary features of a Gothic building, such as piers, buttresses, ribs, mullions and mouldings, assumed a lightness of proportion hitherto unapproached. Gloucester as a great Benedictine Abbey Church would in any case have been in a position to exercise considerable influence with her sister of Glastonbury, and we can well understand how Abbot Monington, in his almost contemporary building effort, was persuaded by the charm and novelty of Gloucester's exquisite work, to attempt an effect of a similar sort in his own choir. The parallel is elsewhere pointed out in detail, but the reader's attention is called to the comparative elevations given in Plates 11a and 11b, shewing two bays of each choir side by side, in which the remnant of Monington's panel-work—still visible in the ragged fringe of masonry attached to the great choir piers—is developed into something like its original propor tions, and its similarity to the Gloucester scheme made evident.

*The east end was not completed till about 1350.

PLATE 3.

VIEW OF INTERIOR, FROM THE NORTH TRANSEPT,

as it probably appeared circa 1500. The drawing is based upon historical data,
but the arch and column in the foreground are assumed as an artistic license in
order to obtain the desired perspective.

So far, we have seen the influence of Wells paramount in the earlier days, modified later by that of Gloucester. The later chapters of the building of Glastonbury present evidence of the continuance of these two influences.

Of the Cloisters, which are stated to have been the work of Abbot Chinnock, 1374-1420, there remain but faint traces, yet these are sufficient to indicate that their design was similar to those of Wells, in regard to the vaulting and the window-tracery, of which numerous fragments have come to light in the course of recent excavation. The date of the Gloucester Cloisters is 1400. The Cloisters of Wells were rebuilt also in the XV century, the eastern walk being the work of Bishop Bubwith who died in 1424, whilst that on the west is Beckington's work (1443-65),

An examination of the external face of the Nave wall at Glastonbury will shew now the later Cloister.

Abbot Bere, 1493-1524, perhaps also felt this influence, since it was he who planned at the East End that great Chapel of King Edgar, which so nearly recalls in its plan and position the Lady Chapel of Gloucester Cathedral.

The final marks of the Wells influence are to be noted also in the works of this Abbot.

In 1338-39 the tower of Wells Cathedral, which was threatening collapse, had been strengthened by the insertion of the three arches known as " St. Andrew's Arches." Abbot Bere, faced by a like emergency about 160 years later, adopted the same expedient, and the Abbey Church of 1500 would have shewn the north and south arches of the crossing braced in this wise. (See Plate   ).

Finally, the building by Bishop Robert Stillington, 1466-1491, of his fine chapel at Wells may have stimulated Bere to the undertaking of the Edgar Chapel, and to some extent also have served as a model, if we may judge from a comparison of certain architectural fragments which yet survive.

We shall now proceed to examine more minutely the Abbey Ruins, and the details preserved to us of their form and enrichments.

PART II.

A Detailed Architectural Survey of the Ruins.

The Chapel of St. Mary the Virgin (commonly called St. Joseph's Chapel).

HIS building, as we have seen, dates from a time immediately subsequent to 1184 A.D., and for about a century afterwards would have appeared as a detached rectangular building, with a turret at each angle, perfectly symmetrical in design. In the chronicle of John of Glaston we read that Radulphus "completed the Church of St. Mary in the place where from the beginning the ' vetusta ecclesia ' had stood, building it of squared stones of the most beautiful workmanship, omitting no possible ornament."

The accuracy of the concluding sentence is strikingly evident in the appearance of the work as it stands to-day. The chapel is singularly rich in ornamental detail, lavishly applied, and yet so well disposed and proportioned that it nowhere appears redundant. The workmanship, too, is admirable. The stone is of so fine a quality that much of the detail is almost as perfect as when it left the carver's hands, and the stones are most beautifully squared, fitted, and surface-dressed,

The architecture of the late XII century is usually described as " Transitional Norman," because it retains to a great extent the massiveness and picturesque detail of the Romanesque or Norman style, but is modified by the new ideas of the " Gothic " builders which when more fully developed in the beginning of the XIII century, gave us our Early English variety of the pointed style.

In this chapel we have an instance of the more archaic type of design, but yet a work representative of the most progressive ideas, and the highest skill and knowledge that its time could afford.

This seems to suggest a desire on the part of the builders to make their work reminiscent of the high antiquity and venerable past of the former church ; and we have little doubt that it was so intended. The regression in style is the more remarkable in view of the fact that the work of Bishop Reginald at Wells had been already well started, having been commenced not later than 1180, and this was purely of the " pointed " or Gothic type, free from any admixture of Romanesque features.

In the Chapel of St. Mary, the Romanesque element is the backbone of the design, whilst the lighter and more delicate detail shews the blending of later forms. The mouldings, for example, are in some cases similar to those used by Bishop Reginald, and correspond both in form and grouping. The chapel does not appear to be altogether of native design, but is more nearly related to a late type of Romanesque found in France. It is very possibly of Burgundian French conception, though to some extent English in its interpretation.

Externally the walls spring from a massive plinth with a broad weathering, resting upon a base mould whose design is purely Romanesque.

Above these the walls are panelled with rich arcades of intersecting semi-circular arches, originally supported upon a colonnade of cylindrical shafts of blue limestone, with carved capitals, moulded bases, and bands of the same material. Internally this feature is repeated, with the addition of carved bosses, beautifully undercut, which appear beneath the intersecting arched head of each division.

The shafts have disappeared, having either been removed by the destroyers, or, what is equally probable, by natural decay. The material is of a perishable nature, and the builders of the chapel were most unfortunate in choosing it, since wherever it remains (as in the capitals of these shafts) it is so decayed that the original beauty of the carving is entirely lost. Had they been content to employ the Doulting freestone, of which the chapel walls are constructed, the design of these carved caps would have been more completely preserved to us ; but we can still gather, by a careful study, something of their original form. They partook of the Early English character, having a hollow bell, and simple foliage typical of that school, with a rounded abacus above. The arcade itself is quite of Romanesque type, with a bold angular zigzag or chevron enrichment, having something the character of the "dog-tooth" of the later period. The intersection of the semi-circular arches gives rise to the pointed form. This type of arcade is habitual in churches of Romanesque design, and was no doubt intentionally contrived in a work like this.

The windows, all of which are placed in the upper part of the walls, will repay careful study on account of the variety and beauty of their detail. The round arch of the earlier period is here retained, but the mouldings are of the refined type associated with the later style, and are magnificently proportioned. The accompanying drawing shews two varieties of the "chevron" enrichment, here developed into manifold forms of beauty.

The windows were originally, of course, each of one clear light, but two or three centuries later they, as well as practically all the wide lancet windows of the Abbey Church, were altered into two-light windows by the insertion of tracery heads, with a central mullion, and transom bar. These fillings have practically disappeared from the four lights on the north and south sides, but some remains are visible at the west end, executed in very inferior stone, and in the last stage of dilapidation. Their historical interest is their sole value, since they detract from the simple beauty of the original design.*

* The same thing has been done at Wells, where a large number of the windows were originally wide lancets. The excessive width made them difficult to glaze satisfactorily without cumbrous metal supports, and this difficulty became greater in succeeding centuries, when the glass employed was thinner, and less fitted to bear the weight and wind pressure. The detail of the tracery fillings in St. Mary's Chapel shew a XIV century character, but it would seem that those in the Great Church were of "Perpendicular" (i.e. XV century) type.

PLATE 4.

ST. MARY'S CHAPEL.

PLATE 5.

NORTH DOORWAY, ST, MARY'S CHAPEL.

The small carved heads at the termination of the label, or drip-mould, over these windows, must be noted, as they are of singular merit, and, in one or two cases, so perfect in form and workmanship as to recall the fine achievements of the early Italian sculptors.

The corbel-table, or row of brackets supporting the parapet, is for the most part missing, but has recently been restored on the south side. Here alone did the old designer miss a possible opportunity for the display of fancy. Romanesque corbels are frequently fantastic in their richness: these are plainly and uniformly moulded, exactly in harmony with those of the great church, and apparently to the same design. In this feature the restrained taste of the later period has conquered the exuberance of the Romanesque school.

The buttresses of the chapel are of singular form. They are Romanesque in type, in that they assume the character of piers or pilasters, set against the wall. The finish at their heads is curious, but obviously incomplete. It has been suggested that the intention of the designer was to represent the roots of trees gathering towards a stem, or clustered group of stems, in the form of light cylindrical shafts running upwards, and terminating in all probability in a foliaged cap at the level of the corbel-table supporting the parapets.

Probably some ornamental terminal occupied the small flat space above the necking, towards which the sides are so curiously gathered.

The angle turrets contain some exquisite design in their upper stages. The small shafts which divide this portion into narrow panels have the peculiarity of blossoming into foliage at the head, without any architectural break, as cap or neck-mould, and are like staves bursting into bud. The pyramidal caps gives us the earliest form of the spire. Upon the summit of these, though now broken, remain the bases of a group of eight small shafts placed as a hollow square for the support of lantern pinnacles, which, when perfect, must have been an element of singular beauty in the general effect.

Of the turrets themselves the two easternmost are solid; those at the west contained staircases. The ancient stair remains in the north-west turret: that on the south-west has been recently restored.

The masonry at this angle was much fractured, and the south wall was falling outwards as a consequence of the violence done by the "Puritanical tenant," who tore down the old turret. On starting the work of repair it was discovered that the foundations at this point had been entirely removed. At the same time that this was done, it is believed that the breach in the centre of the west wall—now filled up —was made, in order that when the turret fell it might bring with it the half of the west wall connected, but fortunately, the schemes of the Philistines were defeated, as the masonry, though wrenched and strained, gave way at another and weaker point, viz., the junction of the staircase.

THE NORTH AND SOUTH PORTALS.

The two doorways of the chapel arrest attention by reason of their richness of detail, and by the skill displayed in the execution of the ornament. The enrichments include foliage, figures of animals, and the human figure. The treatment attains a high artistic level, and is undoubtedly far superior to what is commonly met with in other examples of like date. The portal on the north side is the richer, and was completed by the artist employed, but, unfortunately, the carvings are very much mutilated, and the inner section of the doorway has been removed and is lost, so that, possibly we have not the whole scheme which the carvings were intended to represent. There remain four concentric rings of carved ornament, the outer being filled with sculpture of general character, containing animal forms with foliage work, most beautifully undercut. Next comes a ring carved with a series of medallions, eighteen in number, each containing a figure or figures. The next ring is again filled with purely decorative ornament, finely undercut,* and the fourth, or innermost, shews another group of figure subjects. It is these which must first be described, in order to get the whole scheme in its correct order.

The first two divisions of the group on the innermost ring shew us the Annunciation, the third the Salutation; in

* The 'motif' of the first and third rings appears to be (1) wild or savage nature (3) nature subdued by man, or Christianity. In the outer ring is a well-preserved carving of a wild animal carrying off a man, and in the inner, the representation of a woman milking a cow (possibly Saint Bridget) is still quite clear.

the fourth is the Nativity, in the fifth another subject at present undeciphered; whilst the remaining four panels contain crowned figures, interpreted as being those of the three Kings asking of Herod, "Where is He that is born King of the Jews?"

In the second ring of sculpture, the first seven medallions (starting from the left side) portray the visit of the Magi, who, in the first three, are seen offering their gifts to the Holy Child, seated with the Virgin Mother in the fourth compartment. Then we have the return of the three Wise Men, represented as riding away. The eighth, ninth and tenth panels each contain the representation of a man in bed, and an angel issuing from clouds overhead, symbolising the celestial warning received by the three Magi that they should return to their country by another way. The next four panels (11 to 14) represent the Massacre of the Innocents, and the fifteenth the mourning of the bereaved mothers. In the sixteenth Joseph is warned of the death of Herod, and the last two give us the return from Egypt.*

A brief inspection of the doorway suffices to shew that a member is missing from the head, as well as from the sides. In its complete state the design would probably have exhibited a "tympanum" or flat sculptured stone filling the arch, as well as an additional ring of carved enrichment. The square jambs which stood behind the inner pair of shafts (one of whose capitals is fortunately left to us) are also pulled away, and this has destroyed the true proportions of the opening.

The doorway on the south side retains its five orders or concentric rings of masonry, but two of these—those which would have borne the figures—have never been completed. A commencement had been made of the inner one, and two medallions roughly cut by the artist, but we may suppose that he was called away, and never able to complete his work; and that no one was deemed competent to complete it for him.†

---

* The above description follows that given by Mr. St. John Hope in a communication made to the Somerset Archaeological Society.

† The stoppage of the work in 1189 on the King's death might furnish a reason, and with the accession of Richard, the Crusades began to absorb attention. But the transfer of Hugh from Witham to Lincoln, and the withdrawal of his craftsmen for the great work there seems better to explain the abruptness of the cessation of this work.

45

Allusion has been made to the evidences of French influence in this chapel. These doorways, in form and general character, betray a marked resemblance to some examples to be found in the central districts of Gaul, where flourished a well developed type of Romanesque, very distinct from the northern schools.

The connection between England and France in the XII century was remarkably intimate, and the Church was the strongest link. Consequently we are not surprised to find that at this period France was lending England her best artists and craftsmen.

The influence of Hugh, the Burgundian Prior of Witham, seems clearly manifest in the design of the north and South doorways of St. Mary's Chapel. There was a great church in Avalon of Burgundy, and its western portal is still preserved. It shews five orders of heavy Romanesque enrichment, earlier in date and far coarser in design than that of the English Avalon, but exhibiting a superficial resemblance, owing to the presence of the deep undercutting which is so notable a feature of the English example. The visit of the Magi is there sculptured upon the " tympanum " of the door, and over the group is a canopy of three arches supporting tourelles having a strong resemblance to the same feature visible on the Glastonbury doorway over the " Nativity " group.

Before leaving the exterior of the Chapel, the finely-cut inscription " JESUS MARIA " should be noted on the south wall; also a date faintly visible upon the buttress to the west of the doorway (query 1329) between the rivet-holes for an attached plate.

THE ROOF.

The external form of the roof of St. Mary's Chapel was peculiar, and very rare in this country. It was what is known as a 'hipped' roof—i.e., one sloping on all sides, forming an elongated pyramid, though possibly truncated. Thus there were no gables, but a level parapet all round, with a wide gutter inside approached from the stair-turrets. All the turrets had a clear passage way through them to give access to each side of the roof. The pitch of the roof was

46

PLATE 6.

INTERIOR ST. MARY'S CHAPEL.

ST. MARY'S CHAPEL.

BOSS FROM INTERIOR ARCADE

very high. The exact slope can be seen by looking at the inner sides of the turret at the north-west, where there is a weather-mould built as a protection to the gutters which lay along the junction of roof and wall. Whether the roof covering were of lead or of tiles, there is, of course, no means of ascertaining.

Internally the Chapel was fully vaulted in stone, and the remains of the moulded ribs, with their beautiful 'chevron' ornament still stand. When complete, this roof must have been a work of great beauty, and of a delicacy quite unusual in a period when massive proportions were still the order of the day in spite of the change of style.

INTERIOR ENRICHMENTS.

The carved undercut bosses which are attached to the face of the wall within the recessed heads of the interior wall-arcade are wrought out of the solid stone, but so exceedingly perfect is the undercutting, and the finish of the surface, that they scarcely appear to be a part of the wall. Here and there they have fallen away, leaving a smooth surface, on which are visible the minute points of contact which were all that the carver retained.

With these arches too, are very distinct traces of fresco, in the form of cuspings with foliations. Collinson says that in his time pictures of saints were also discernible on these walls.*

THE FLOOR AND CRYPT.

As originally designed, the interior face of the walls footed upon a bench table or stone seat around the three sides of the chapel and thus formed a series of shallow stalls divided by shafts of lias limestone, four to each bay.

There was no crypt or basement in the original design. Any doubt on that point was set at rest by the examination of the footings this year. They are quite shallow. The subject is ably and exhaustively dealt with by Professor Willis in his ' Architectural History ' of the Abbey,

---

*Beauties of British Antiquities (1779), pp. 216—229.

The crypt of this chapel, being a work of the XVI century, will be more conveniently dealt with when we come to describe the works of the later epoch. It will be sufficient here to say that all the subterranean features, including the door and steps leading down to it, and the various windows cut through the plinth of the chapel, are foreign to the original design, in which the floor was at the ground level or thereabouts,* and the fine bold plinth swept without break or interruption (save for the two doorways north and south) around the whole circuit of the walls.

THE WELL.

The well, though connected with the later crypt, is undoubtedly much older, and may perhaps have been the baptistery of the older church.

It is not clear how this well was originally covered. The richly moulded arch of XII century date which now protects it does not appear to have been really designed for the purpose, but is almost certainly formed from the heads of the semi-circular windows which were set in the old east wall of the chapel and pulled down in the XIV century to allow the Galilee to be united with the chapel. The detail, if compared with the semi-circular heads of the windows remaining in the west wall, will shew this.

THE GREAT CHURCH.

ITS PLAN AND DIMENSIONS.
(SEE PLATE XII).

In the Charter of King Henry II we learn that Radulphus laid the foundations of a church 400 feet in length and 80 in breadth Whether these dimensions were external or internal is not said, and in any case they would scarcely be more than approximate, as such general directions can never be rigidly enforced in the execution of a complex work of many features, such as a large mediaeval church.

*The ancient floor, we are told, was of stone, incised with geometrical figures inlaid with lead.

48

The width of the existing building, within the walls, does not exceed 75 feet. The choir walls are about six feet thick in their lower part ; and the south wall of nave, upwards of eight feet.

When we come to examine the length of the existing church, it is more difficult to trace the 400 feet originally spoken of. Taking as a datum, or fixed point, the square of the central tower, which is under 40 feet from centre to centre of the piers, and, assuming that the 'Galilee' was a part of the original scheme, we should obtain figures approximately as under, the dimensions being internal or clear dimensions.

	Feet.	Ins.
The Galilee or Narthex (including doorway to Nave)	59	7
Nave of nine bays	186	6
Square under central Tower	39	3
Choir of four bays	78	8
Retro-choir	36	0
	400	0

But the plan of the church as it now stands, is so altered from what its first builders laid down, that the original scheme is hardly in evidence.

We have in the existing church, the following series of interior dimensions, which, added, give us the total clear length of the buildings, within the walls.

West to East.	Feet.	Ins.
St. Mary's Chapel with Eastern Arch ..	59	2
Galilee with threshold of West Door of Nave	59	7
Nave wall face, to east face Transept ..	224	0
Length of Choir and Retro-choir to face of East wall	153	9
Edgar Chapel with passage way, to east wall of Apse	83	6
(Approx.) ..	580	0

Allowing for thickness of walls at each end of the building, with buttress, plinth, or other projections, we obtain a grand total of 590 feet, or thereabouts, as the clear length of the Abbey. The length given by Queen Elizabeth's Commissioner, appointed to make a survey of the buildings about 1560,* is 594 feet, but this appears to have been meant for an internal measurement, and, as such, is demonstrably inaccurate.

ARCHITECTURAL FEATURES.

The fragments which remain of the transept walls, with the choir piers, and chapel walls adjoining, also the isolated fragment of the south aisle wall of the nave, give us, in their practically unaltered character, a clue to the original XII century design ; whilst the walling of the choir aisles for the first six bays eastward is of the same date.

We have no evidence as to how far the work had proceeded when it received a check of 50 years duration, on the death of Henry II ; but the aisle walls, in the uniform appearance of their masonry, suggests a continuous work. and are likely to have been erected during that period. We see in the detail of all these fragments the same proportions, and their unity of architectural character is remarkable.

The nave was of nine bays, or arches, the pillars on north and south being of solidly grouped or clustered shafts,

---

*Nothing more contradictory or perplexing than the figures given by writers on the Abbey could well be conceived. Collinson, the Somerset historian, and John Carter, quoting older authorities, give 220 feet as the length of the nave from St Mary's (Joseph's) Chapel to the base of the tower pillars, and 45 feet for the breadth of the tower, equal to the *cross isles* (i.e,, transepts), the choir 155 feet—making the total from east to west 420 feet, to which must be added the length of St. Joseph's Chapel, given by Carter as 110 feet, so that their total within the walls will be found to be 530 feet, whereas the actual measurement is just under 500 feet in the clear.

In the plan given by Professor Willis, the nave measures 201 feet, and is of ten bays. In that which was published in September, 1904, by the Royal Archaeological Institute, the length is 191 feet, and there are but nine bays to the nave. This is correct. Willis's general plan gives a total internal measurement, by scale, of 520 feet : but this includes a small eastward projection for a chapel, The Archaeological Institute's plan of 1904 omits all projections at the east end, and limits the length to about 500 feet. Finally we have the traditional length of 580 feet given by older authorities, which is proved correct by the discovery of the Edgar Chapel.

Several recent publications have repeated the old mistake of giving the nave ten bays, or arches, whereas there were but nine.

as we may judge from the appearance of the responds attached to the west wall.

The same design appears in the fragments which yet remain of the responds in the choir, and the shafts in the transepts. These grouped shafts are a feature of the later style, and are found at Wells, of a very similar type, in the work commenced by Bishop Reginald, A.D. 1180. We have in Wells the pattern for this much, at least, of the early design of Glastonbury, and it is plain that Bishop Reginald, who consecrated the Chapel of St. Mary in 1186, may have had a good deal to say in the matter of the Glastonbury work.

The nave piers at Wells, though similar in plan, are somewhat smaller than those of Glastonbury, which appear to have reached a breadth of nearly eight feet from east to west.

The lozenge-shaped foundation of one of these piers, recently uncovered in the choir, measures 11 feet diagonally across the footing ; and the actual measurements of the shafts themselves can with sufficient certainty be reconstructed from the portions of the piers yet remaining in the transepts.

The lancet windows, with their equilaterally arched heads, and unusual breadth of proportion, have also a strong likeness to those in Reginald's work at Wells, though the original simplicity is there disguised by a later insertion of Perpendicular mullions and tracery. The windows of Glastonbury were furnished with similar features, but these have fallen out, with the exception of some remains in the west lights of St. Mary's Chapel,

Other parallels to Bishop Reginald's work may be found in the moulded corbel blocks which supported the parapets ; but these are much bolder and finer at Glastonbury.

The architectural scheme of the Abbey externally seems to have been simplicity itself, and to have partaken largely of the character of the architecture of the reformed Benedictine communities of France.

The influence of Cistercian ideals of building, which shew an austere beauty and perfect interpretation of constructional principles, is here unmistakably visible. The plan of the great church also, with its eastward transeptal chapels, and its Galilee at the west end of the nave, reflects the same influence.

Glastonbury was a Benedictine House, and the Abbey church was built just at the time when a great movement of reform in matters religious was going forward ; and side by side with this a new and more perfect type of architecture was being developed.

The Galilee, together with the west end of the Nave, was the last part of the original church to be built, but the long suspension of the building works causes us to see a complete change of style, in this portion—which is of late XIII century type.

But this difference in architecture does not imply any change of plan, and we have no evidence which would entitle us to assume that the " Galilee " was an afterthought.

On the contrary, all the evidence is on the other side. To begin with, an examination of the north wall of the Galilee clearly shews that it is not a separate structure, but is built in unison with the great west wall of the nave. Then the word "galilee" which we know was of old applied to this particular building was one of very ancient significance and described a feature which was customary in churches of this class until as late as the end of the XII or beginning of the XIII century, though it fell into abeyance after that time.*

The plan of Glastonbury in this respect follows the lines customary in many great Benedictine churches of France. At Pontigny it is proportioned somewhat as here, but is flanked by side chapels.   At Clairvaux and Citeaux it is of greater breadth, and covers the ends of the aisles.†

Our own Cistercian Abbey of Byland shews the remains of such a building, there known also as a " Galilee," and it appears also at Fountains and Rievaulx, whilst in Ely Cathedral it appears in the form of a western transept, as well as a western porch.‡   Peterborough shows a modification

---

* The word implies an outward division, corresponding to the Court of the Gentiles in the Hebrew Temple, and this outer division is to be found in most early churches where it was most anciently allotted to penitents, catechumens, or others who had not full privileges of church fellowship.   (At Durham it was a Porch of the Women).   It is otherwise known as the Narthex, and, with the Nave and Sanctuary, make up the symbolic *tripartite* division of ancient churches.

† The Galilee or Narthex was greatly developed in Burgundian churches, where it was sometimes of enormous size.   The Benedictine Abbey churches of the XI century at Tournus and Fleury both possess one.

‡ See Stewart's "Ely" p.p. 50, 56.   This author favours the theory that the Ely Galilee consisted originally of the two western transepts with the space connecting them (beneath the Western Tower).   The old fabric rolls speak of the North and South Galilees.   The porch is a later addition.

of the idea, in the great space beneath its three arched portals, and Wells, possibly, in the *exedrae* under its western towers. But the nearest parallel to the Galilee of Glastonbury is that of Durham Cathedral, where it covers the west door of the nave.

As at Glastonbury this was originally built as a Porch, but (again like Glastonbury) was found convenient for use as a Lady chapel, its more ancient use having become obsolete. At Durham the legend of the dislike of Saint Cuthbert for the fair sex was made to explain the transfer to the west of the Altar of Saint Mary (frequented by women). No such excuse was needed at Glaston, for here the chapel of the Blessed Virgin had subsisted from time immemorial and what more easy, or more natural, than to throw down the barrier which parted the galilee from the chapel, and let it be absorbed ?

But it is quite clear that these galilees were not originally contrived as lady chapels, and their conversion to this use would be nothing more than a local expedient.

To return now to the architectural features of the nave and transepts, we observe that everywhere an enrichment is employed of the "chevron" or "zigzag" type, and in this respect the building is unlike Wells, but follows another influence—that of a school under which the Cathedral of Saint David's was erected. This work was started in the same year that Reginald began his nave at Wells, and was therefore also standing as a model for Glastonbury. It exhibits in similar variety almost the identical patterns we find at Glastonbury, though less boldly and effectively proportioned.

This blending of traditions is very striking, and seems without doubt intentional, and designed by the builders to symbolise that union and reconciliation of different races and their churches for which Glastonbury stood. Saint David's, representing the old native church, contributes an architectural element which is brought into beautiful harmony with the work of the English school, as typified by Wells, and underlying these we seem to see the thought and stimulating power of Hugh, the Burgundian, soon to be the greatest of English cathedral builders.

The part of the church first to be completed was the central area, as we have seen in the foregoing "Chronicle."

Evidence of its greater antiquity seems presented in the character of some of the chevron work in the transepts. This is specially in evidence in the small arch to the south of the great choir opening where the ornament is of a quite simple Romanesque or Anglo-Norman Type. [Compare this with the later variety in the corresponding position on the north]. This simpler chevron is also visible in the return arches just inside the choir, leading into the side chapels. It appears quite reasonable to suppose that the debris of Herlewin's church may have yielded a quantity of quite uninjured masonry enrichments, and that these were used up as far as they would serve, by the builders of the new church, who, it is clear, were above all things desirous of perpetuating the links with the former time. The zigzag on the little choir arch in the south transept wall appears to be worked in a different stone, and has a more weathered surface than the surrounding masonry—which seems to give corroboration to this view.

At Saint David's Cathedral the nave arches are semi-circular and those of the presbytery, pointed. We might perhaps infer a similar difference at Glastonbury from the fact that the "drop" arch inside the nave aisle windows has the semi-circular form, which here bespeaks no difference of date, but a deliberate variation of design.* The actual window heads of the Glastonbury work are pointed, but are hardly visible from the nave, as the windows are set very high in order to clear the cloister roof.

The half of the cloister doorway yet remaining also seems to have had a semi-circular arch, and it will be noticed that here again the simpler "zig-zag" is used, shewing that in all probability the lower part of this wall was early built.

The design of the interior faces of the main divisions of the Glastonbury transepts is easily to be re-constructed from the fragments remaining (Plate IX) and satisfies the most critical sense in its perfect balance of proportion. The idea of carrying up the heavily moulded arch on continuous shafting, to overtop the triforium arcade, has the singular merit of combining

---

* The "zig-zag" enrichment in the choir is far more in evidence than it is in the nave, where it alternates with plain mouldings in the window arches. In the cloister door it is feeble in contrast to the corresponding enrichment in the great arches of the triforium, and others in the region of the transepts, which are very large in scale.

these two stages, which otherwise would have presented the disconnected appearance seen in other great churches, and which somewhat detracts from their impressiveness. The triforium at Glastonbury, at all events in the transepts, was not used as a passage for its whole extent, *but the circuit of the walls, and the approach to the belfry was by means of a clerestory gangway, the ends of which, together with the spiral stairs in the choir piers to the tower over, still exist.

The Early English detail of the triforium is of great beauty. The trefoiled headstones of one of the arcades have been recovered, and are now incorporated in the north transept. The clerestory detail is equally fine, and both stages were furnished with shafts of blue lias with finely carved foliaged caps of the same material, as we find in St. Mary's Chapel. Attached to the wall are ornamental bosses, finely carved, and undercut with great boldness.

The upper parts of the Choir walls were originally of similar character to those of the transepts, but have been refaced and completely altered by Monington.

The triforium and clerestory of the Nave are believed to have been the work of Abbot Geoffrey Fromond (1303—1322), and of his successor Abbot de Sodbury.

The five eastern bays of the vaulting in the south aisle of the Nave follow the earlier design in their section, having the double roll, and the vaulting of the east part of the Nave itself, which we are told was the work of Abbot Fromond, probably followed suit.

Abbot de Sodbury completed the vaulting of the Nave, and may be deemed to have made a further departure in style, since we can see such a marked change in the vaulting springers remaining against the aisle wall at the point where he took on the work.†

Abbot Fromond was probably responsible for the building of the greater part, if not the whole, of the upper

---

* It stopped a short distance from the tower piers where the return face of a doorway can still be seen, giving access to the space behind the triforium.

† They shew square nosings and chamfers in place of the double roll. The springer of the cross-rib at this point rises perpendicularly for several feet, instead of curving outwards in the normal manner. This would have made a curious hollow break in the surface of the vaulting.

parts of the Nave walls. We have unfortunately nothing of
his work standing, but it is reasonable to infer that whilst
agreeing in its general proportions with the original scheme,
the detail employed would be that which was characteristic of
his own period.

The study of fragments of stonework remaining in the
Abbey grounds suggests the treatment of the Nave Triforium
recalling that of Wells Cathedral (see annexed figure).

The ball-ornament is here used as an enrichment, and
it is also visible in certain fragments of the vaulting ribs
having the double roll.

PLATE 7.

THE ABBEY RUINS.

(View from Choir, looking towards Nave.)

PLATE 7A.

THE SAME, SHEWING CONJECTURAL FORM OF NAVE, &c.

NORTH PORCH.

Nothing now remains above ground on the north side of the nave to indicate the existence of a north porch, and up to the present time (1910) no examination of the foundations has been made at this point.

But there are distinct reasons for believing that such a feature existed, and of these the most conclusive is to be found in William Wyrcestre's description of the church.

This writer mentions an entrance porch to the great church 45 feet long by 24 feet wide ; and he, writing in Latin, speaks of it as—"*Anglice* a porche." An attempt has been made to shew that he meant the galilee, but this is very unconvincing, because long before William Wyrcestre's day, the galilee, at all events in its western part, had become the *choir* of the lady chapel. Besides, the internal length of the Galilee is not 45, but 52 feet,

William Wyrcestre, moreover, gives the dimensions of the galilee in another place, incorporating them with those of the Chapel of St. Mary, regarding them as a single building—thus :

"Longitudo Capella B.V.M. quae est contermina ex parte occidentale Navis Ecclesiae 34 virgas × 8 virgas " (the length of the chapel of the Blessed Virgin, which adjoins the west end of the nave of the church, is 34 yards by 8 yards in width).

The influence of Bishop Reginald's work at Wells on the original design of the church at Glastonbury lends support to the idea that a north porch might here have occupied a similar position. Willis points out that this would bring it opposite the principal gateway which, according to Hollar was the one on the north side of the Abbey.

THE WEST END OF NAVE.

The likeness to the design of Wells is again apparent in the arrangement of the west wall, with its two trefoil-headed recesses on each side of the doorway, but here the style is later and the proportions are different, the size of the doorway much greater than at Wells, and the side-panels less. Over the head of this door ran at one time a narrow gallery or passage supported on corbels, of which two still remain in the moulded head, whilst the sockets of several others are visible in the rough masonry.

This wall was carried up for some distance to the cill of the west window in order to clear the galilee roof. All evidence of the design of the window is gone, but to carry out the Wells parallel we might expect to find three lancets with trefoiled heads, something after the manner indicated in Plate 7, in which this wall is seen from the further end of the church.

The depressed segmental arch to the west door on this side is suggestive of a later period, but it is a genuine Early English work.*

The inner ring of masonry which held the doors is now missing. There were probably two doors, with a shaft between (sketch) which is the usual arrangement, and one of the symbolic features of a church described by Durandus, a XIII century writer.

Towards the Galilee, this doorway assumes a much grander aspect, and when complete must have been a magnificent feature. Over the doors were canopied niches for statutary, filling the

West Face of Portal to Nave.

tympanum, and on the wall on the right, a moulded bracket still shews where a statue stood, probably for a votive altar.

The ashlar face of the wall on this side runs south past the line of the south wall of the galilee, shewing that there was a passage through the wall at this point, with a door, most probably leading into the turret staircase of which the hollow curve is still visible in the rough masonry of the west wall. The remains of a similar staircase can be traced even more

* Compare the fragment of the flat internal arch to the 12th century doorway leading to the cloisters.

clearly on the north side, but this one was entered from the nave, and there are indications that a passage may have been taken off this staircase at a higher level into the Galilee,* through an archway taking the place of the last of the three windows in that compartment of the north wall, which appears to have been covered by the tower.

The remains of this arched head shew a chamfer and rebate like those of the windows of the period, but above these appears a plain rear-arch which seems to stamp this as a doorway. Hence it has been deemed more prudent not to follow it in the conjectural reconstruction of the exterior form of the windows given in Plate 10. The effect of this arch, if developed as an external feature, would be peculiar, and from its heaviness scarcely in harmony with the rest of the work.†

WESTERN TOWERS.

The presence of the two spiral staircases, which are of large diameter, indicate the existence of large turrets at the north-west and south-west angles of the nave.

A careful inspection of the rough masonry outside the wall on the north side of the Galilee shews that the projection of the turret was so great as to cover about a third of the first bay ; whilst there are evidences of a heavy plinth of masonry like that of Wells, forming the foundation of the turret.

In this we see presumptive evidence in favour of Western Towers as a part of the original scheme, but a more convincing point in support of this theory is that indicated by Mr. St. John Hope, namely, that the western bay of the nave is shewn by measurement to have been broader by about four feet (east and west) than the rest, and this can only mean that the masonry of the last pier of the nave was thus broadened to give support to a heavy weight over, viz., that of a tower. During the autumn of 1908 a careful examination of the footings at the south west extremity of the nave was made, and revealed the fact that the external

---

* Possibly for access to an elevated pulpit or tribune.

† For the details of the lights shewn in Plate 10, and the quatrefoil ornament over, no claim is made beyond the requirements of good proportion, and the character demanded by the period of the work ; in particular, the height of the centre light of the triplet must remain a matter of conjecture.

wall is also broadened to the south, being brought out beyond the line of the nave wall to a projection of about two feet. This gives the proportions of the tower, and the evidence, taken together, may be regarded as conclusive.

The footings of the stair-turret at the south-west angle of the nave, of about equal size to that on the north, were found. The foundations also of a massive buttress on the west face of the south-west tower were revealed. It stood approximately half way between the angle of the Galilee wall and the outer angle of the nave. Its presence here was corroborative of the existence of a heavy tower at the south-west angle of the nave. It is hoped that a similar excavation on the north side may reveal corresponding features. Evidence of the former existence of these towers in local tradition is supplied in the MS. Diary of John Cannon who speaks of " ye great tower in ye middle, lofty, now nothing left of it," and " also two smaller towers on ye north and south sides,"

THE GALILEE.

This building was erected in a mature Early English style, the mouldings being those used in the later years of the XIII century. The original design showed three separate windows in each of the three divisions of the walls north and south. These were presumably of equal height outside, as we see by the trace of their original heads in the wall ; but internally the side lights were lowered to clear the vaulting. Thus the appearance would have been somewhat as shewn in the drawing [Plate 10]. Some time late in the XV century, for what purpose we do not know, unless it were to secure stability when the crypt was constructed, these lights were removed, and the thickness of the solid walling increased, a single window (probably of three smaller lights with narrow mullions) being substituted. The beautifully carved corbel course was retained in position. The Galilee in its original state was a fragile work, not capable of withstanding an onslaught upon its foundations, such as occurred in later years, when the crypt was excavated.

The features of the building were slender, the mouldings delicate. The fillet replaces the keel, on the rounded members. The canopied buttress on the south side gives us a clue to the real intention of the design. It is modelled on Jocelyn's work in the west front of Wells. Provision is made for statuary in the hollow sides of the buttresses. Blue lias shafts were largely used here, and each salient angle held one. The windows in the original scheme were similarly treated.*

The west front of the great Church being co-eval, and its internal resemblance to Wells so apparent, we may legitimately infer that the exterior design of the Tower walls followed suit with the Galilee in recalling Jocelyn's magnificent conception.

The beautifully moulded head of the doorway on the north side of the Galilee must not be overlooked. The fall of the buttress on the west of it, due to the depredations of Thomas Prew or John Down, have caused the collapse of the keystone, and the spreading of the tympanum, with a loss of true proportion, which cannot be restored until the buttress has been once more set upright in its original position.

Formerly this door and another on the opposite side gave access to the Galilee when it was a Galilee or *porch* ; but when the crypt was formed, the floor was raised, and they were no longer available as doorways.

Early in the XIV century the east wall of the Chapel of Saint Mary was thrown down, and the arch formed which is now visible in a restored condition, so that the Galilee became as it were a chancel to the Lady Chapel. There is no record of the date of this alteration, but a benefaction of Abbot de Sodbury (1322—1335) is recorded, which provides endowment for a daily Mass in the Lady Chapel, and is regarded both by Willis and Parker as implying that the union of the two buildings had probably been effected in his time.†

* There are some charming little undercut bosses built in the outer face of the XV century masonry fillings of the Galilee wall, very like those in St. Mary's Chapel (interior arcade). They came without doubt from the inner faces of the old Galilee walls, and are thus shewn in Plate 10.

† *ex* John of Glaston (Hearne) p. 268. "He assigned to the office of the Sacrist XX marcs annually for the maintenance of four priests well skilled in singing, who, together with the two anciently appointed *to the Galilee*, and the other two are supplied by the sacrist and the almoner, shall daily perform the service, with melodious singing *in the Chapel of the Blessed Virgin*, clad in surplice and amice, and shall come in the same manner to the solemn masses of the choir." The vaulting of the Galilee was probably the work of Abbot Adam de Sodbury, who completed that of the Nave, and we might assign 1330 A.D. as a conjectural date for the arch between the Galilee and St. Mary's Chapel.

THE PLAN.

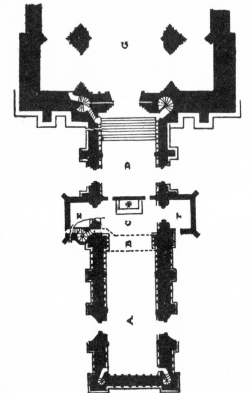

A St. Mary's (the Lady) Chapel.
B Arch, and probable position of Roodloft.
C Portion of Galilee forming Choir or Presbytery of Lady Chapel, showing conjectural position of Altar and Altar Screen.
D Eastern portion of Galilee with doors of access to Nave of Abbey Church (G).
E Conjectural site of the Biconel Chapel, with spiral staircase to the Roodloft.
F Chapel or Sacristy (of which indications survive).

NOTE.—The dimensions of E, F, are conjectural.

The staircase at the east end of the Galilee would make it necessary to keep the principal altar some little way back, and there would probably have been an altar screen, or reredos wall with side doors, across the chapel, to the westward of the north and south doors of the Galilee, which at this date were not blocked by the raising of the floor level, since this took place nearly two centuries later.

There was also in all probability a Roodloft over a screen which stood beneath the archway dividing St. Mary's Chapel from the Galilee which had become its chancel. There are distinct traces of a spiral staircase at the north-west corner of the Galilee, immediately adjoining the north-east turret of St. Mary's Chapel, and the curved face of the staircase may be seen leading inwards towards the upper part of the Galilee wall, which must have been penetrated by a small opening at this point, although the wall recently re-built does not shew this.

LATER FEATURES OF
THE GALILEE AND ST. MARY'S CHAPEL.

THE CRYPT. THE WELL AND STAIRCASE. CHANTRIES.

It has been shewn that St. Mary's Chapel anciently had no crypt. Neither, it is quite clear, had the Galilee, The foundations of the latter building are certainly carried much deeper, and under the eastern bay they have been examined, and found to go down to the level of the crypt floor—but the softness of the ground at this point, and the absence of marl rock at the customary level, furnish good reason for this care, to say nothing of the precautions needed in building this comparatively light structure in union with the heavy mass of the west wall of the church. The difference in settlement may be seen on the north side, where the heavier and the lighter masses have separated and cracked apart. Under this point the old masons inserted a relieving arch in the wall, which makes the foundations of the two massess practically independent.

63

The crypt of the Galilee was first to be excavated, probably about the year 1500. It would appear that the architect of this part did not disturb the Chapel of St. Mary till this work was completed. The crypt extended beneath the two western bays of the Galilee, and was limited on the west by the foundation of the east wall of St. Mary's Chapel.

The form of the vault is curious, as the curve is not continuous to the crown, where the intersection is quite flat for a considerable distance. It will be seen that the voussoirs, or vaulting-ribs, are of Norman character, and that the shafts of the piers on which the vault rests are formed of similar material. It seems obvious that old material of early XII century date has here been used up, and it is quite reasonable to suppose that this was done intentionally to assist in perpetuating the ancient character of the place, possibly to create an impression on the minds of the pilgrims who frequented the shrines here that the crypt was itself of high antiquity. In the ribs are seen the series of holes made for the suspension of the chains of hanging lamps. The caps and bases of the little shafts against the wall are cut in a rude imitation of early work, but the caps are clumsily designed, and of quite nondescript shape (A, in sketch).

The eastern section of the Galilee, which is beneath the steps to the Nave door, was never dug out, as an examination of the ground has proved: and it is evident from the rough finish of the vaulting ribs at this end that no continuation was thought of in this direction,

It must have been very shortly after the completion of the crypt under the Galilee that the extension beneath St. Mary's Chapel was formed. The latter differs chiefly from the first in having vaulting of its proper period—late Perpendicular, as the surviving indications prove; and the imposts are also of the later type, those at the west end being quite of the Tudor pattern, whilst the rest (B, in sketch) shew the springers of the diagonal vaulting ribs of the later style neatly worked into an arch-mould of Norman design, copied from the section of the pier below.

The two strainer arches of rough stone now crossing the chapel are modern, and were inserted by a late owner as a support for the walls, which were tending inwards.

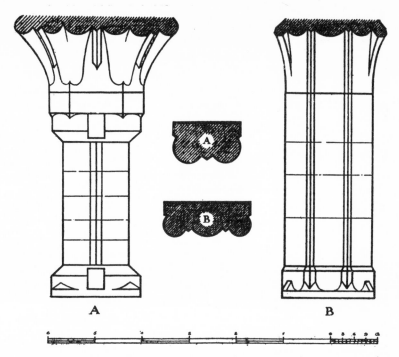

A   B

As the chapel crypt extends eastward to meet the portion under the galilee, it occupies the position beneath the former east wall of the chapel—and thus is longer by six feet than the chapel itself. Consequently its four divisions are each about eighteen inches longer than the divisions of the walls in the chapel over—and thus the piers are not in line. The floor of the crypt was of plain hexagonal tiles (see portion remaining). A barrier or screen divided the two eastern bays from the rest, and there is evidence of a bench of wood having been run around the walls in the western part, as the responds are mortised near the ground.

The windows of both crypts are of the same late style, with flat arches over their reveals on the inner face of the wall, but in the Galilee these arches have a large moulding in imitation of the Norman work. The reveals of all the windows are arched over with a vault that slopes upwards and outwards to such a degree that it has been possible to place the window frames in the basement moulding of the chapel. The back walls of these recesses slope back to give more light, and to act as a retaining wall.

Professor Willis has noted the fact that these vaults are sunk much deeper than Norman crypts, which were usually planned to allow of one-third, and sometimes one half, the height of the crypt to be clear of the ground. At Glastonbury the crown of the vault is level with the ground. The entrance to the crypt is at the north-west corner, by a late Perpendicular doorway. The steps are modern. When the old steps were first discovered by Mr. Reeves, in 1825, they were found quite broken and useless. Mr. Reeves removed them, and excavated about fifteen yards north, under the present foot-path, where no less than eighteen coffins were found, all of oak, two or three inches thick. Under the head and shoulders of each corpse was placed a bundle of wood shavings. Beneath, and on the right side of the skeleton, was a rod of hazel, of the same length as the coffin. Three at least of these interments were undoubtedly older than the crypt. One of the skeletons was 8 ft. 3 ins. in length.

Mr. Reeves also cleared the crypt, which until 1826 was full of earth, and he also brought to light the well, the existence of which had long been forgotten. It is approached by a passage about 17 feet long, of which the entrance alone was perceptible prior to the clearance of the crypt.

The passage to the well was formed at the time the crypt was constructed. Here we have a late Perpendicular doorway, and a ribbed vaulting over the head of the passage of the same date.

The arch over the well has exactly the same character as the window heads at the west end of the chapel, and is in all likelihood formed of those which came from the east wall of the chapel when the XIV century builders took it down in order to include the Galilee. The well itself stands quite clear of the footings of the north-east turret. Previous to the formation of the crypt it must have been approached independently, either by a flight of steps from the cemetery, or as there is some reason for supposing, by a subterranean passage from the south. The orifice of this passage is believed to have been in the south wall of the well enclosure, at the foot of the newer stair, and is remembered by persons still living in Glastonbury. It was blocked up and the cavity filled by the owner of the property upwards of fifty years ago on account, it is said, of the loss of lambs which occasionally fell into it.

In the XVI century there stood a sacristy or chantry against the western bay of the wall of the Galilee on the south side, just east of the wall, and we have evidence of a doorway pierced at this point. The newel stairs from the well probably turned east, and by a cross flight over the head of the well passage entered this sacristy, A branch flight led up into St. Mary's Chapel through the little doorway still existing, whose pretty canopied head on the inner face of the wall must be noted. The steep zig-zag steps now leading from this, down to the well, are modern.

On the north side of the Galilee a similar late appendage was built against the wall, and this was no doubt the chapel mentioned by Leland as the burial place of John Biconel and Elizabeth his wife.* Traces of a wall jutting northwards from the base of the N.E. turret of St. Mary's Chapel are still visible, and some scanty remains of the footings of a return wall running east and west, some little distance north of the main wall, were brought to light in excavation in the spring of 1910. This probably marked the northern limit of the chapel. Adjoining it on the north was a deep water-channel with a shallower one lying beside it at a higher level. Formerly there was no facing on the Galilee buttress on the eastward side, and it was consequently an open question whether the east wall of this small chantry had not been incorporated with it ; but in the recent restoration of this buttress no account has been taken of this possibility, since an uniform ashlar facing has been given it.

Another building of late date covered the wall at the north-west angle of St. Mary's Chapel, on the north face. The grooves cut in the original wall for its lead gutter-flashings mark its height. The purpose of such a building we can but conjecture. The pilgrims frequenting the shrines in the Crypt probably needed a place of assemblage, where they would rest, and be marshalled. The detached angle of walling of XIV century date remaining belongs to another building lying westwards from this point. It appears to have been vaulted. Part of the walling on its south side was standing early in the XIX century, and shewed an arcading of interlaced traceried heads, apparently of XIV century date, harmonising in appear-

---

* "In Capella S. Mariae, a Boreali parte Chori in Sacello: i.e., in the Chapel of St. Mary, from the north part of the *choir*, in a small chapel.

ance with the chapel walls. The extent of the foundations is not yet known. Between this angle and the turret of St. Mary's Chapel was a wall with a doorway parting the cemetery of the laity, which was north of the chapel, from that of the monks, which was on the south and west.

THE CLOISTERS.

These stood against the south aisle wall of nave, and were returned against the west wall of the south transept. Together with the returns, they covered seven bays of the aisle wall, there being two bays of the cloister to each one of the nave, and the length of their northern side, from east to west, works out at 142 feet, divided as follows :—

Width of west walk ..	..	13 ft. 0 in.
End bay (west) ..	..	14 ft. 10 in.
8 intermediate bays at 10ft. 2in.		81 ft. 4 in.
End bay (east) ..	..	14 ft. 10 in.
Width of east walk ..	..	13 ft. 0 in.
	Total	137 ft. 0 in.

The east walk was about 131 feet long, as follows :—

Width of north walk ..	..	13 ft. 0 in.
9 bays at 10 ft. 2 in.	..	91 ft. 6 in.
Add for walling at ends ..		2 ft. 0 in.
One do. (under) at 13 ft. 3 in.		13 ft. 3 in.
Width of south walk ..	..	11 ft. 6 in.
	Total	131 ft. 3 in.

The cloister floor was at a level of four feet below the nave floor and most of the east walk has now been exposed to view. Recent excavation has also shewn the bases of the responds which stood against the walls dividing the bays, and the marks of the rivets or cramps by which the upper parts were attached are visible.

The cloisters, which are believed to have been the work of Abbot Chinnock (1374-1420) were vaulted in stone, and the detail now recovered indicates a similarity to those of Wells. The flooring was of encaustic tiles, and they had windows of richly painted glass in fine stone tracery. The line of their arches can still be traced against the aisle wall, and at the apex of each is a little sinking for a boss. The curve of the ribs is shewn by the grooves visible, and there are remains of the cement fillings behind still adhering.

The two rows of shallow square sinkings which run all along this wall have been described as the marks of the monks' "carrils" or bookshelves, but they are not so. These shew the position of the rafters and gutter beams of the older wood-roofed cloisters which Abbot Chinnock's work superseded. The lower range, which took the feet of the rafters, is nearly nine feet above the cloister floor.

On the face of the wall above are visible the skewbacked corbels which formed the apex of the flying buttresses, carrying the thrust of the nave vaulting outwards over the cloisters.

THE FLOORS OF NAVE AND TRANSEPTS.

The grass level is practically that of the old nave floor, which is raised about nine feet above the clay at the west end, and about six feet above the level of the more ancient church which it superseded. We learn from the antiquaries of the XVIII century that there were vaults beneath the *body* of the church, and it is probable that by this expression the nave is meant. A deep trench cut down the centre of the nave at the west end revealed no sign of a vault, but shewed the foundation wall of an older church just inside, and parallel to, the west wall of the nave ; and traces of a concrete floor at a depth of six feet or thereabouts.

The floor of the nave appears to have been flagged, and there is very little appearance of tiles in the debris. The transept floors, on the contrary, were almost certainly tiled over their whole area, and the excavations everywhere yield plentiful fragments. In the early days of the XIX century an area of 8 ft. by 6 ft. of perfect floor-tiling was uncovered in the transept chapel, and was for some time on view, but all traces of it are gone. During the spring of 1909, however, in the course of levelling the grass bank, a perfect fragment was found "in situ," and this gives us the true level of the transept floor. The rise from nave to transepts is approximately 4 ft.

The tiles discovered exhibit a striking variety of designs, including several kinds of scroll patterns, some of an unusual type, shields charged with chequer work or lions rampant ; two-headed eagles, birds pecking fruit, and lastly a very interesting representation of a three-towered church, which may possibly have some reference to the actual design of the Abbey Church, though this, like all the rest, is a local variation of a conventional pattern employed by the tile-makers of the period. The tiles are mostly of the XIV or early XV century, of red clay with shallow pattern grooves filled in with white clay, giving, when glazed, a brown and buff, or olive and buff, surface. Some tiles of XIII century and yet earlier date have also been formed.

TRANSEPT CHAPELS.

The floors of the transept chapels were raised, and part of the stone curb forming their threshold is now visible in the north transept. These chapels were probably screened in stone. Each was furnished with a stone altar, and recessed piscina with drain for the washing of the chalices, in their south walls. The stone walls were covered with a thin film of plaster, painted over with an uniform rectangular jointing, each rectangle containing a small red rosette at the centre.

The chevron enrichments of the arches opening into the transept chapels were of great beauty, to judge by the specimen remaining, and the foliage of the caps extremely well designed. There is a cap in the chapel on the south side which shows an enrichment derived from the lopped branch shewing its ring of bark—a feature seen in great variety at St. David's, where it is treated in a most ingenious manner, and shews every stage of evolution from the purely imitative to the highly conventionalised and decorative type.

FEATURES OF THE CROSSING.

The great piers of the choir arch still shew the grooves made by the masons for the admission of the fluid cement which united the ends of the overhanging vaulted canopies of Abbot de Tautonia's great choir screen to their faces. This screen would have exhibited a central doorway, and probably an altar on each side, following the customary arrangement, as still seen in its entirety at Glasgow Cathedral. It supported the " pulpitum " or loft on which the choir organ was placed, and which sometimes had a rostrum or pulpit-like

PLATE 8.

VIEW THROUGH CHOIR LOOKING SOUTH.]

projection facing westward. Over this screen, according to the records, would have been the Rood, before which Abbot de Tautonia was buried.

The difference in level between nave and transepts must have necessitated the presence of a flight of eight or nine steps, beneath the great western arch of the crossing, some forty feet westward of the choir screen. This arrangement precisely recalls that of Canterbury Cathedral.

There must have been a heavy central tower at Glastonbury, since the piers bear marks of violent pressure, and have bulged and broken their foundations. About 1500 A.D., Abbot Bere, who put in a stone vaulting beneath the tower, like that of Wells Cathedral, and very probably added something to the height and external grandeur of the tower itself (as the mere addition of the vaulting would scarcely account for the partial collapse of the great piers) was compelled to brace the two great transept arches by the insertion of "Saint Andrew's Crosses," *i.e.*, inverted arches, on the same principal as those at Wells, which were erected in 1338. But his work, being 160 or 170 years later, was of course lighter in design, and we have an excellent clue to the pattern, in one of the central junction stones which occupied the intersection of the four arched arms. This still lies near where it fell, on the north side, and is by good fortune well preserved. It shews some excellent mouldings. The semi-octagonal base of Bere's arch on the south rests in its ancient position and on both choir piers we can trace the line where his work impinged upon the older masonry and took its pressure, whilst we can see where he cut away the double shaft and carved caps which originally stood against the west face of the pier, following the design of those in the choir opening. Plate 3 shews a conjectural reconstruction of Bere's inverted arches

The Choir.

This was originally of four bays, similar in character it is believed, to those of the transepts. Monington, who became Abbot in 1342, proceeded to carry out an elaborate scheme of alteration ; and there is no doubt that he was influenced by the famous work in the Benedictine Abbey of Gloucester, whose choir was in process of being remodelled about 1337-40 A.D. Having already a work of considerable refinement for the basis of his design, he did not, as at Gloucester, mask the whole surface, but was able to preserve the beautiful clustered pillars and the arcades with their fine enrichment. What he did was to cut away the great arches over the triforium with the wall surface above them overhanging the lower part, and reduce the whole to an uniform thickness. Then he applied to the whole height of the walls above the choir arcade a network of beautiful panelling, dividing each bay into four principal compartments, and twice as many minor ones. The two middle compartments of the four were pierced, and glazed, and these became large windows, but they were on the inner face of the wall, and consequently the old lancet lights on the outer face of the wall became superfluous.

Monington, however, suffered these to remain. He merely took out the glass, and lowered the cills about four feet, lowering, at the same time the roofs of the triforium spaces, and the marks of these changes can be seen still on the outside of the choir walls.

The choir, after his reconstruction must have presented a peculiar appearance externally, as the lancet windows would have been seen as dark cavities, without glass, and the actual windows, which were much wider, were a couple of feet inside them, the walls being splayed out to admit the light to the whole area. Leland tells us that each of these great windows contained six panels. The manner in which this description applies may be seen by referring to Plate 11a, in which two bays of the choir wall are reconstituted from surviving fragments. The ragged fringe of Monington's work still remaining attached to the east side of the choir piers, slight though it be, is sufficient to make it possible to reconstruct with a fair degree of certainty the main lines of his scheme : though some of the features in the drawing here given, *e.g.*, the tracery pattern in the heads of the windows, and the design of the vaulting, are necessarily conjectural.

The vaulting, as shewn in the plate, is adapted from Monington's two models, viz. : the work of Ralph de Salopia in the choir of Wells, and that in the choir of Gloucester (11b). Both these works undoubtedly influenced him.

It will be noted that the springers of the vaulting ribs of the first bay of the choir still remain, and these shew the same double roll of the earlier type which seems to have been used by Abbot Fromond in the east part of the nave. There are several varieties of this member preserved among the fragments. Some shew the hollow between the rolls enriched by a ball ornament—others shew pateras in the shape of flowers, and again we have one exceedingly beautiful variety with an undercut scroll of foliage, uniting the rolls. But their origin is uncertain, and some no doubt refer to the aisles of the choir, or the retro-choir. There are also sections of vaulting of a more advanced XIV century character in the Abbey, with smaller and more complex mouldings, uniting at various angles, with bosses at their intersection, shewing traces of elaborate carving. It is a roof of this nature which probably covered the eastern prolongation of Monington's choir, and this we have indicated in the drawing. Abbot Monington appears to have followed the example of Gloucester in having embarked in some rather daring construction at the East End as we may judge by the remains of the massive double buttresses provided by him in the aisle wall. His design probably included a large East window, below which were three arches, and immediately in front of these stood the High Altar, on a platform 20 ft. x 12 ft. The foundations at this end were uncovered in 1908 and the situation of the pillars of the three arches in the east wall of the choir was noted. Between them was a continuous foundation, indicating either a reredos wall, or the position of the former wall of the old retro-choir, when the church was shorter.*

Just in front of the High Altar platform a deep channel was discovered, running diagonally from the south aisle wall (where a low arch is drawn in some of the old engravings) in a north-westward direction, and this was traced as far as the centre of the choir.

THE AISLES OF THE CHOIR.

A peculiarity of the plan is visible in the second bay of the choir walls from the west, where the chapels of the transepts jut forward and half obscure the windows. Here the difficulty

---

* Foundation walls almost in line with this were found to run across both aisles, and there was evidence of buttressing in connection with that on the north side.

E

has been neatly overcome by dividing the window openings verti-
cally down the centre, allowing the western half to be filled with
masonry, whilst the eastern half opens out to an angular "squint"
for the admission of light to the aisle within. The first six
bays of the aisle are in the original style of the Abbey work,
but in the fifth and sixth we see an alteration in the level of
the vaulting, which is here raised some four feet. This would
appear to indicate an original intention to raise the floor level
at this point for a corresponding height. But the same floor
level was continued further east, as we see by the bench table
against the wall which runs on to the middle of the sixth bay,
where it ceases to be a part of the wall. The three narrower
bays beyond are of a later period, built (probably by Abbot
Monington) to form a new rectro-chapel to the eastward of the
lengthened choir. The old style has been followed in the
main, but the details of the caps and bases of the responds
attached to the inner face of the wall is later, and is quite of
Monington's period. The double roll is retained for the section
of the vaulting ribs, and doubtless these shewed one of the
ornamental features previously described (*i.e.*, ball-flower
pateras, or scroll-work.)

The floor of the retro-chapel was originally a little
higher than that of the choir, as we see by the lifting of the
bases of the responds, and just where the bench-table ends,
there was probably a step intended, but there must have been
a change of plan after the walls were built, and the same level
was carried through to the east wall, the bench-table being added,
though not bonded into the wall.

Attached to the outside of this wall were one or more
buildings of later date, either sacristies or chantries. There
was certainly a doorway under the window of the third bay,
and it is probable that there was another under the fourth.*
Outside the third bay the string course and basemould had been
cut away, and the walls grooved for the reception of a lead
flashing. The foundation trench of a small building has been
revealed in the ground outside.

---

* The whole of the fine masonry under the cills of these two windows was torn out by
  the destroyers in the XVIII century. The effect can be seen in part in the
  coloured frontispiece. The present ashlar filling on the inner face is the work of
  one of the more recent owners. Its extent can be traced by the fact that it does
  not carry on the line of the string course under the cills.

The narrow seventh bay corresponds to the thickness of the east gable wall, and above the responds the wall is thickened for the base of a massive turret or pinnacle provided to give stability to the twin flying buttresses which here over arched the choir roof, and carried the thrust of its vaulting down to the large pair of buttresses on the outer face of the aisle wall. These buttresses are of Abbot Monington's date, and were obviously designed to give support to some special feature of construction at the east end,

Similar twin buttresses, and of a like date, are provided on the eastern return wall in line with the choir arcade. They are hardly explainable as a mere architectural feature, and we may conclude that they also carried flying buttresses to the angle of the east wall of the choir above, so that there would be, in all, four such pairs of buttresses, two pairs attached to the north-east angle of the clerestory, and two to the south-east.

This would imply a work of a rather ambitious character at the east end, light or fragile for its size, and again we look to Gloucester, where the whole east wall is a huge window, and wonder how far Abbot Monington may have taken this marvellous feature as his model.

These buttresses are very substantial, but none too solid for the work they had to do. They served their purpose for about 150 years when, according to Leland, the east wall had begun to " cast out " in so threatening a manner that Abbot Bere was obliged to add more buttresses. As those that Monington built bear no trace of later workmanship, we must look elsewhere for Bere's additional supports.

THE RETRO-CHOIR.

This part contained an ambulatory or processional way, with five chapels to the eastward. The position of the walls dividing the two outer chapels from the rest is clearly seen in the fragments of the east wall remaining, but of the two inner division walls no trace above ground is left, and it was not until the summer of 1908 that their existence and position was verified. The missing walls were of curious design, and some record is preserved in J. Britton's 'Antiquities' Vol IV.

They were exposed in 1812-13 and roughly sketched. At that time they were thought to be part of a crypt, perhaps owing to their rude or heavy character, but it has been found that their foundation goes no deeper than that of the rest of the walls, and as the nature of the ground shews, no crypt could ever have existed here.

The two piers indicated in Britton's plan are apparently of massive character, and are in an isolated position, at some distance from the east wall of the retro-choir. From their somewhat crude form in the drawing they give the impression of being simply the foundations of a work of more architectural character, which probably took the form of a pair of clustered shafts united on their eastern sides to traceried stone screens dividing the three central chapels. This is to be inferred from a sketch in Kerrich's Diary, preserved in the British Museum.

As to the number of chapels in the retro-choir it will be seen that the position of the internal walls gives room for five, and this is the number given by William Wyrcestre in his XV century notes.* Previous writers have endeavoured to shew that these were but four chapels, and the position of the altar in the second chapel from the south has been cited as a proof of the correctness of their view, since it was placed apparently so far from the wall on the south that, if centrally placed, it would demand a chapel of a width extending to the centre line of the main building, thus making four only. But the altar back is not complete, and just below the grass there remain on the south side a further sixteen inches, which entirely alters the whole calculation.

The chapel in question, i.e., the one just south of the central one, had clearly a width of rather under 12 feet, and allowing the same for that on the north, the balance of space left for the central chapel or passage way is considerable, the whole clear width being 39 ft. 4 ins.

In Monington's time, the central chapel of the five would appear to have projected beyond the line of the rest for a distance of 12 feet or thereabouts, precisely to the point to which Abbot de Sodbury's earlier lady chapel would have extended.

* To the east of the high altar are five columns in a row, and between each, a chapel with an altar. This writer counts the two responds or half-columns at ends, as together making one column; a method he also adopts in describing the nave arcade.

Certainly Monington's central chapel did not terminate in an uniform line with the rest, since the foundation of the east wall of the retro-choir did not cross the central space, and the virgin clay lies close beneath the surface at this point.

At a point 12 feet further eastward, however, there exists a deep trench in which lies a massive wall, now seen as the west wall of the Edgar chapel. Moreover the footings of the projecting side walls of this chapel are clearly marked in the clay, and correspond in depth and in width also with those of the east wall. But the end of this chapel was knocked out by Abbot Bere in the XVI century, when he turned it into a passage way or staircase to his new chapel of King Edgar.

THE EDGAR CHAPEL.

The foundations of this chapel were re-discovered by the author in the summer of 1908 and have now been fully opened up, and the necessary repairs effected. They had been lost to sight for generations, and so completely forgotten that antiquaries had come to regard the old fragments of the East wall of the Abbey as the extreme limit of the building, and the possibility of finding any further extension had been denied.*

The chapel was originally rectangular, but there are two additions, probably by Abbot Whiting, one of which takes the form of a small polygonal apse, and the other a shallow chantry or sacristy on the south side.

The foundations laid down by Abbot Bere are very massive, the side walls being 6 ft. 6 ins., and the end walls 4 ft. 6 ins. thick. The junction walls to the choir are thicker again, but these are probably the older walls, and they, together with the west end wall of the Edgar chapel, lie at a much deeper level than the rest, A channel for the drainage of surface water is formed in the walls around the whole circuit of the chapel and is connected with drains running through the Abbey grounds westward. Three inspection holes have been formed in the footings, in which these channels may be seen. The clear area comprised in the rectangular foundation

---

* Eyston mentions in his list of chapels "St. Edgar's, at the East end, back of the Choir, commenced by Abbot Bere, and completed shortly before the Dissolution of the Abbey." It was customary in recent years to regard this chapel as being merely one of the series of five in the retro-choir.

of the Edgar chapel is 50 ft. by 18 ft. 6 ins   This would give a rather greater length, and a considerably greater width for the chapel itself, since according to the custom of the later builders the side walls would certainly be deeply bayed internally, so that the probable dimensions of the chapel itself, before the addition of the apse, would be about 52 ft. x 25 ft.

The buttress footings are very massive, and project about five feet, shewing that a roof of heavy construction needed to be supported. They divide the chapel into four equal bays of 12 ft. 6 ins. each.

There is a considerable mass of rough masonry remaining at the east end, and this, at the south east angle, reaches a height of close upon eight feet above the choir grass, shewing that the floor of the Edgar chapel must have been laid at a yet greater height, since all this walling has the character of underground walling.

The apse foundations are exceedingly shallow, and commence at a level some six feet above the rest. The walls here are much thinner, and the masonry (remains of which may be seen on the south side) inferior to the other. The apse appears to have been of three faces with sloping sides. The angle of these side walls is about 67° with the lateral axis of the chapel, giving a rather acute semi-hexagonal form. The end wall is missing, having been removed, it is believed, about 1812, together with the remains of the tile floor of the apse. They were near the surface of the ground, which has since been raised. The absence of the east wall makes the form a little puzzling.

The appearance of the apse walls is rendered yet more irregular by the fact that the foundation of the south wall has been increased in thickness in order to accommodate a drainage channel, and hence spreads fan-wise towards the centre of the apse. But this irregularity of thickness would scarcely have extended higher than the covering of the drain, and the section of walling remaining at a higher level is of uniform width with the trench on the north side whose position is now marked by a wall.

Between the last two buttresses to the east, on the south side of the rectangular part of the chapel appear the foundations of a small additional building, either a chantry or a sacristy. These again are shallow and narrower than the main work.

The total length of the Abbey Church internally is given by the older antiquaries as 580 feet, and a careful measurement of this distance from the west wall of Saint Mary's Chapel, brings us precisely to the point within the apse, required to give it symmetry. As the east wall has been removed, it has not hitherto been thought desirable to make any reconstruction, since the evidence, however strong, was of an inferential nature. But in the summer of 1910, the required proof was forthcoming, and this is of a nature to lift the matter once for all out of the region of controversy, and place it in the category of established facts.

An XVIII century manuscript, found in a private collection, gives the precise dimensions of this chapel, 87 feet being stated as the length beyond the choir, and this is exactly what is required to make an apse of perfect form, giving a clear internal length to the Abbey of 580 feet, in accordance with the statements of Hollar, Hearne, and other antiquaries of the older time.

The chapel is described in this manuscript as 'King Edgar's Chapel,' a fact which may be commended to the notice of certain antiquaries of renown.

In Warner's " Glastonbury " (p. lxxxvii.) an inventory is quoted, extracted from a M.S. of early Elizabethan date, in which a general series of dimensions of length of the Abbey church is given, but until recently this has not received full consideration, owing to the fact that the chronicler has, in ignorance or inadvertence, miscalled the Edgar chapel · the "Chapter-House," thus misleading all students, as the Chapter-House was of course in quite another situation. The entry is as follows:—

"The great church in the Aby was in length 594, as followeth :

The Chapter House, in length   90 foot.
Quier, in length   ..   159 foot (in breadth 75 foot.)
The bodie of the Church
                   in length 228 foot.
Joseph's Chapell, in length.. 117 foot.
                              ―――
                              594

This total, if the measurement in question was meant for an external one, might be reasonably correct, but the individual measurements given are very inaccurate (compare table p. 49), and are mostly in excess of the actual ones, which make the total approximately 580 feet.

During the excavation of this chapel a large number of interesting architectural fragments were brought to light. These include stained glass, encaustic tiles, and a variety of freestone mouldings, with some carved detail. A considerable quantity of this was painted with vermilion or black, and gilt.

The character of the fragments is quite corroborative of the date assigned to the work, viz. : early XVI century. Two of the most important fragments were from the vaulted roof. One is a section of the vaulting, shewing the panelled fan-work of the period, and the other a heavy carved boss or apex stone, shewing the intersection of twelve moulded ribs. These indicate a roof of the nature of that in the chapel of King Henry VII at Westminster, though of course hardly so elaborate as that masterpiece of Tudor masonry.

The discovery of the Edgar Chapel makes Glastonbury Abbey the longest ecclesiastical building in England, but one longer being recorded, namely, Old Saint Paul's, which was stated by Dugdale to be 690 feet in total length but this measurement, taken from Stow's Annals (Strype's Edn. Vol. i, p. 640), has been shewn to be a mistake. The true length, as circulated by Mr. Ferrey, works out at 590 feet. (See Hist. of the Three Cathedrals of St. Paul's. Wm. Longman, F.S.A., Lond, 1873,)

Chart of the Building

of

Glastonbury Abbey.

A.D.	BUILDER.	WORKS EXTANT.
708	Church of King Ine.	? Foundation under West of Nave.
946	Dunstan, Abbot.	? ditto ditto.
1082—1101	Turstin, Abbot.	? Fragments in walling under Nave.
1101—1120	Herlewin, Abbot.	(1) Angle of walling under Nave (probable).
		(2) Traces of walling of apsidal form under crossing of Abbey Church (probable).
		(3) Burnt stones in walling of later Church, recognised by their red colour.
		(4) Chevron moulding (early) in S. Transept arches.
		(5) Voussoirs in Crypt of Galilee (?)
1126—1171	Henry de Blois, Abbot.	Bell Tower (foundations not yet located).
1171—1178	Robert, Abbot.	A Chamber and Chapel (not located).

1184. A.D.—THE GREAT FIRE.

[CONTEMPORARY BUILDERS.]

1174—1191	Reginald Fitz-Joceline, Bishop of Wells.	Nave of Wells Cathedral commenced about A.D. 1180.
1175—1186	Hugh of Avalon, Prior of Witham.	Witham Priory Church built.
1176—1198	Peter de Leia, Bishop of St. David's.	Nave of St. David's Cathedral commenced A.D. 1180.
1186—1200	Hugh, Bishop of Lincoln.	Lincoln Cathedral building.
1184—1189	Ralph Fitz-Stephen appointed Steward.	Chapel of St. Mary built, and consecrated. 1186-7 by Bishop Reginald.
	No Abbot for seven years.	Great Church partly built, the central portion first started. Walls probably built to Aisle height, and the earlier Cloisters erected.
1189	Death of King Henry II. Death of Ralph.	
1191	Death of Bishop Reginald	Work stopped.
1191—1193	Henry de Soully, Abbot (or Swansey). William Pyke, Abbot.	No building attempted.

F

CHART OF THE BUILDING 1192—1334.

A D.	BUILDER.	WORKS EXTANT.
1192—1205	Savaric, Bishop of Wells.	Abbey involved in wrangles and disputes. (Savaric, Bishop of Glastonbury 1193—1205).
1206—1242	Jocelyn Fitz-Trotman Bishop of Wells.	West Front of Wells Cathedral built.
1206—1218	Jocelyn Fitz-Trotman Bishop of Glastonbury.	Abbot T. B. Snow states in the 'Downside Review' for December, 1890. (p. 195) that St. Mary's Chapel was completed in 1216.
1218—1223 1223—1234	William Vigor, Abbot. Robert de Bath, Abbot.	No building work recorded.
1235—1255	Michael de Ambresbury, Abbot.	Erected many monastic buildings and probably continued the building in the Choir and Transepts of the Abbey Church. (Buried in the North Transept.)
1255—1260 1260—1274	Roger Ford, Abbot. Robert Petherton, Abbot	No building works recorded.
1274—1291	John de Tantonia, Abbot.	The Choir of four bays completed, and the West end of Nave and Galilee built.
1278	Visit of Edward Ist and his Queen.	The bones of King Arthur placed with great ceremony before the High Altar.
1291—1303	John de Cantia, Abbot.	This Abbot furnished the completed Choir and its Altars.
1303—1322	Geoffrey Fromond, Abbot.	This Abbot spent £1,000 on building. The Central Tower was completed and the Eastern part of the Nave vaulted. The Great Hall of the Monastery began. The Abbey Barn probably erected.
1322—1323	Walter de Tantonia, Abbot.	Caused the great Choir Screen to be built.
1323—1334	Adam de Sodbury, Abbot	Completed the vaulting of the Nave, united the Galilee to St. Mary's Chapel and endowed a Daily Mass. Gave the Abbey Clock and Bells, the great Organ, etc. (Buried in the Nave.)

CHART OF THE BUILDING 1334—1524.

A.D.	BUILDER.	WORKS EXTANT.
1334—1342	John de Breynton, Abbot	Completed the Great Hall, made minor gifts to the Church and St. Dunstan's Shrine.
1342—1374	Walter de Monington, Abbot	Lengthened the Choir by two bays, and re-faced its interior, built the Retrochoir, and vaulted the whole of his work. Built the Western half of the Chapterhouse, and sundry other works.
1374—1420	John Chinnock, Abbot	Rebuilt the Cloisters, and completed the Chapter-house. Finished works left incomplete by Monington, and erected the Dormitory and Fratry.
1420—1456	Nicholas Frome, Abbot	This Abbot probably built his Abbot's Kitchen, but his predecessor had been credited with the work, by some authorities.
1456— 1456—1493	Walter More, Abbot } John Selwood, Abbot }	No building works in the Church recorded.
1493—1524	Richard Bere, Abbot	Built the greater part of the Edgar Chapel, erected the vaulting beneath the central Tower, and probably added to the Tower itself ; causing a partial collapse, which he remedied by inserting "St. Andrew's Arches" under each Transept Arch, as at Wells. Excavated and built the Crypt under the Galilee and Chapel of St. Mary. Added Flying buttresses to the East end of the Choir. Built the Loretto Chapel after his journey to Italy. This Chapel was attached to the North side of the Nave. Built a Chapel of the Holy Sepulchre at the South end of the Nave. Also the Almshouses and Chapel on North side of Church, the Manor House of Sharpham, and new apartments in the Monastery for priests and for Royal Guests.

CHART OF THE BUILDING 1524—1539.

A.D.	BUILDER.	WORKS EXTANT.
1524—1539	Richard Whiting, Abbot.	Completed the Edgar Chapel. [Including, probably, the apsidal extension and a small Sacristy at the south-east corner, which are obviously both later additions].
		Said to have greatly improved the Monastery.
		[The Abbot's House, seen in Plate I, appears to have the character of a late piece of work and may have been erected by either of the last three Abbots].

Appendix.

The following is the original text of the Declaration of Royal Supremacy as preserved in the public records, together with the signatures of the Abbot and his Monks. It will be seen that the scope of the Document is far wider than a mere acknowledgment of the King's Headship, and that not only is the claim of Papal jurisdiction over the Church in England expressly repudiated but it is resolved that in any conference the Bishop of Rome shall no longer be called by the name of Pope and that none shall petition him as Pope, but as Bishop of Rome. The divine law in the sacred Scriptures, and the laws of England, are to be maintained against all such laws, decrees, and canons of Rome as are contrary to them. No one of the signatories shall hereafter presume to turn anything taken from the Sacred Writ in any alien sense, but each one binds himself to preach Christ and his words and acts in simplicity, openness, and sincerity, according to the norm or rule of the Sacred Scriptures, and of the truly Catholic and orthodox Doctors.

Each one further pledges himself that in making his customary prayers and supplications, he will commend to God and to the prayers of the people first of all the King as Supreme Head of the English Church, next the Queen, etc., and lastly the Archbishops of Canterbury and York with the rest of the Clergy in their proper order.

The attestation of this document by the Abbots, Priors and Monks of the great religious houses of England* has been interpreted by Papal apologists as an act of weakness. This is equivalent to a wholesale charge of perjury, since it would involve a total insincerity in the oath taken.

The act, if one of mere weakness, would indicate a cowardice and subservience in matters of principle impossible to men of stable character; if insincere, then surely an act of the direst hypocrisy. Is it possible for any man of fair mind to consider that all these communities of devout men could merely by force of compulsion have been induced to forswear falsely their allegiance to the rule of a Divinely-appointed Head at the bidding of a temporal authority? Such a suggestion is simply unthinkable.

---

* See Rymer's 'Foedera,' Vol. XIV.

TEXT OF THE DECLARATION

(From the Chapter House, Westminster)

Quum ea sit non solum Christiane religionis et pietatis ratio, sed nostre etiam obedentie regula Domino regi nostro Henrico Octavo, fundatori nostro prexcellentissimo cui uni et soli post Christum Jesum servatorem, nostrum debemus universa non modo omnimodam in Christo et eandem sinceram integram perpetuamque animi devotionem fidem et obedientiam honorem cultum et reverentiam prestemus sed etiam de eadem fide et observancia nostro rationem quotienscunque postulabitur reddamus et palam omnibus si res poscat libentissime testemur. Noverint universi ad quos presens scriptum pervenerit quod nos Ricardus Dei patientia Abbas Monasterij beate Marie Virginis Glaston Bathon. et Wellen. diod. et ejusdem loci conventus uno ore et voce atque unanimi omnium concensu et assensu hoc scripto nostro sub sigillo nostro communi in domo nostra capitulari dato pro nobis et successoribus nostris omnibus et singulis imperpetuum profitemur testamur ac fideliter promittimus et spondemus nos dictos abbatem et conventum et successores nostros omnes et singulos integram inviolatem sinceram perpetuamque fidem observantiam et obedientiam semper prestituros erga dominum regem nostrum Henricum Octavum et erga Annam reginam uxorem ejusdem et erga sobolem ejus ex eadem Anna legitime tam progenitam quam progerandam et quod hac eadem populo notificabimus predicabimus et suadebimus ubicunque dabitur locus et occasio. Itemque confirmatum ratumque habemus semperque et perpetuo habituri sunt quod predictus rex noster Henricus et Caput ecclesie Anglicane. Item quod episcopus Romanus qui in suis bullis Pape nomen usurpat et summi pontificis principatum sibi arrogat, non habet majorem aliquam jurisdictionem a Deo sibi collatam in hoc regno Anglie quam quivis alius externus episcopus. Item quod nullus nostrum in ulla sacra concione privatim vel publice habenda eundem episcopum Romanum appellabit nomime Pape aut summi pontificis sed nomine episcopi Romani vel ecclesie Romane et quod nullus nostrum orabit pro eo tanquam Papa sed tanquam episcopo Romano. Item quod soli dicto domino regi nostro et successoribus suis adherebimus et ejus leges ac decreta manu tenebimus episcopi Romani legibus decretis et canonibus qui contra legem divinam et sacram scripturam aut contra jura hujus regni esse invenientur imperpetuum renunciantes. Item quod nullus nostrum omnium in ulla vel privata vel publica concione quicquam ex sacris scripturis desumptum ad alienum sensum detorquere presumat

sed quisque Christum ejusque verba et facta simpliciter aperte sincere
et ad normam seu regulam sacrarum scripturum et vere Catholicorum
atque orthodoxum doctorum predicabit catholice et orthodoxe. Item
quod unusquisque nostrum in suis orationibus et comprecationibus
de more faciendis primum omnium regem tanquam supremum caput
ecclesie Anglicane Deo et populi precibus commendabit deinde
reginam Annam cum sua sobole tum demum archiepiscopos Can-
tuariens. et Eboracens. cum caeteris cleri ordinibus prout videbitur.
Item quod nos et omnes et singuli Abbas et Conventus predicti et
successores nostri conscientie et jurisjurandi sacramento nosmet
firmita obligamus quod omnia et singula predicta fideliter imperpetuum observabimus. In cujus rei testimonium huic scripto nostro
commune sigillum nostrum appendimus et nostra nomina propria
quisque manu subscripsimus. Dat. in domo nostra capitulari decimo
nono mensis Septembris anno regni regis nostri Henrici Octavi
predicti vicesimo sexto.

Monasterium Beate Maria Virginis Glaston. in Com : Somer's.

19 September 26 Henry VIII.

P'me Ric Abbas	Nicholas Andrew	Robt. Yder
Nichola' Londo. p'or	Johes Arthur	John Oswolde
Nichola' Wedmor	Johes Abaramathia	Jo. Pauly
Rob Clerk	Willm Dustane	Jacobus Anselmus
Johes Towton	Wlls. Kentyne	Johs Elphege
Thomas Dustone	Johes Deryvyan	Wyllm Adelwoldus
Thos Clem	Marvul Judratt	Symon Edgar
Johes Selwood	Laurenci' Maur	Johs Phaga
Johes Bennett	Galfridu' Bennyg	Johes Pantales
Johes Bennyg	Walterus Herstan'	John Allends
Richard' Bede	Ricard' Wuscet'	ArystothlesAlvyrn'
Johes Ceolfryde	Johes Excet'	Richard Rabone
Thamas Appollynar	Wyllms Joseph	Thomas Brentt
Henricus Yvo	Johs Baptista	Henry Mowntegeld
Ricus Besill	Johes Ambros'	Johes Aldelme
Robt' Glyde	Rychad Ulton	Roger Wylfryd
Johnes Verney	Wyllam Brythwold	
Edmud' Cokere	Johes Aydan	

(These names are copied from the original document in the
Public Record Office.)

BIBLIOGRAPHY

"Glastonbury: a study in Patterns." No. 1. 1969. R.I.L.K.O.

"Britain: a study in Patterns." No. 2. 1970. R.I.L.K.O.

"Occasional Paper No. 3." "Sacred Geometry: The Proposals of Frederick Bligh Bond at Glastonbury Abbey." Reviewed 1979 Keith Critchlow.

"Gematria." Bligh Bond and Simcox Lea, 2nd Edition 1977 R.I.L.K.O.

"The Apostolic Gnosis." Simcox Lea and Bligh Bond, 2nd Edition 1979. R.I.L.K.O.

"The Gate of Remembrance." Bligh Bond, 5th Edition 1978 Thorsons, Wellingborough, Northants.

"Time Stands Still." Keith Critchlow 1979. Gordon Fraser, London.

Glastonbury Abbey Poster: a geometric lay-out with leaflet. Elizabeth Leader and Keith Critchlow 1975.

"Theon of Smyrna: mathematics useful for understanding Plato." 1979. Trans, Robert and Deborah Lawlor.

Index.

PLATE 9.

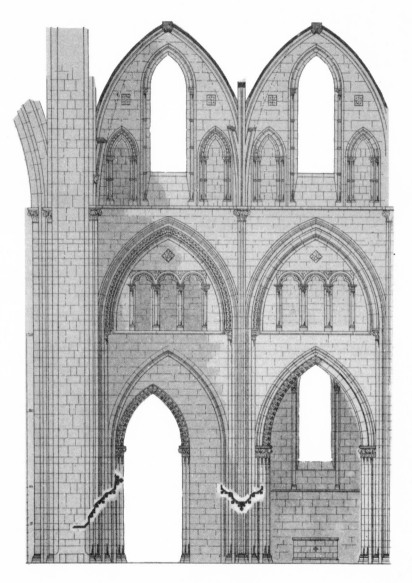

GLASTONBURY ABBEY.
Elevation of Two Bays of South Transept.

PLATE 10.

One Half Exterior.　　　　　　*One Half Interior.*

THE GALILEE.
Conjectural Reconstruction of one Bay of North Wall according to
the original (XIII Century) Design.

PLATE IIa.

GLASTONBURY ABBEY.
Conjectural Elevation of Two Bays of Abbot Monington's Choir.

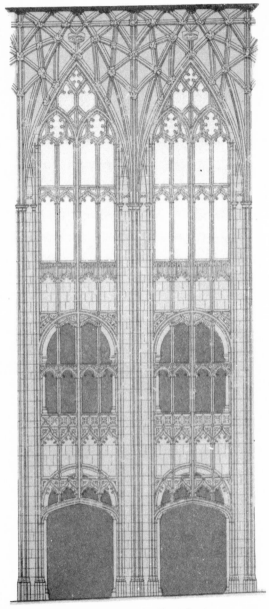

GLOUCESTER CATHEDRAL.
Elevation of Two Bays of the Choir.